first
names

Dwayne
'THE ROCK'
JOHNSON

Lisa Williamson

Illustrations by Tammy Taylor

KU-797-153

First Names: DWAYNE 'THE ROCK' JOHNSON
is a
DAVID FICKLING BOOK

First published in Great Britain in 2022 by
David Fickling Books,
31 Beaumont Street,
Oxford, OX1 2NP

Text © Lisa Williamson, 2022
Illustrations © Tammy Taylor, 2022

978-1-78845-175-8

3 5 7 9 10 8 6 4 2

DAVID FICKLING BOOKS Reg. No. 8340307

A CIP catalogue record for this book is available from the British Library.

Printed and bound in Great Britain by Clays Ltd, Elcograf S.p.A

The facts in *First Names: Dwayne 'The Rock' Johnson* have been carefully
checked and are accurate to the best of our knowledge, but if you spot
something you think may be incorrect, please let us know. This text is
intended to be entertaining, that's why we've included Dwayne as a cartoon
character. However, the words and thoughts spoken by this character are
not the words and thoughts of the real Dwayne Jonnson – they're
sometimes just for fun – and the Explains sections aren't explained
in Dwayne Johnson's own words.
Some of the passages in this book are actual quotes from Dwayne and other
important people. You'll be able to tell which ones they are by the style of
type: *I had seven bucks in my pocket. That's when I made a choice.*

Dwayne 'THE ROCK' JOHNSON

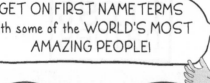

GET ON FIRST NAME TERMS with some of the WORLD'S MOST AMAZING PEOPLE!

Technological powerhouse and innovator

Feisty women's-rights campaigner

High-flying feminist icon

Death-defying escape artist

Teenage activist for girls' rights

The woman who made coding cool

The man who abolished slavery in the US

Gifted, globetrotting Portuguese pioneer

The most intelligent man who ever lived?

Superwoman and superstar

World-famous freedom fighter

Unstoppable climate activist/campaigner

★ CONTENTS ★

INTRODUCTION	7
1 - DWAYNE'S ROCKY START	12
2 - HURRICANE DWAYNE	33
3 - DWAYNE FALLS HARD	42
4 - DWAYNE HITS ROCK BOTTOM	51
5 - DWAYNE IN THE RING	57
6 - BAD-GUY DWAYNE	85
7 - DWAYNE HEADS TO HOLLYWOOD	99
8 - DWAYNE TAKES CONTROL	109
9 - DWAYNE - ACTION MAN	116
10 - BUSINESSMAN DWAYNE	136
WRESTLING TERMS	148
TIMELINE	150
GLOSSARY	152
INDEX	153

INTRODUCTION

THE PLACE: Honolulu, Hawaii
THE TIME: 1986

Fourteen-year-old Dwayne Johnson yelled goodbye to his mum and let the door slam shut behind him. He headed out onto the street as usual and found himself pausing to gaze up at the luxury apartment block across the street. Shiny and imposing, it dwarfed the modest three-storey building where he shared a cramped studio with his parents.

'One day,' he thought. *'I'm going to live somewhere like that.'*

Deep down, Dwayne knew the odds weren't in his favour. He wasn't very serious about school, often skipping classes to hang out with his friends and cause trouble in the neighbourhood. He'd already been arrested several times for petty crimes like shoplifting and vandalism. If Dwayne wanted to live in a big fancy apartment one day, he needed to get his act together and fast.

Later that same afternoon, Dwayne came home to find his mum standing outside their apartment. He was confused. Why wasn't she inside? As he got closer, he realized she was crying. As soon as she saw Dwayne, she tried to put on a brave face, but it was too late – her cheeks were already streaked with tears.

'What's wrong?' Dwayne asked, panic rising in his chest. 'What are you doing out here?'

With a trembling hand, Dwayne's mum pointed at a sign pinned to the door.

'It's an eviction notice,' she explained, fresh tears brimming in her eyes. 'We have to leave right away.'

That's when Dwayne noticed the padlock on the door.

He'd always known money was tight. Just the week before, his mum's car had been repossessed and they were behind with their rent yet again. However, he'd had no idea things were this bad.

As his mother sobbed, Dwayne hugged her to his chest and made a decision. Instead of stealing, getting into fights and causing her all kinds of stress and worry, he was going to channel his energy into something else, something positive. He was going to try to make a success of his life and make his dream of living in a fancy apartment a reality.

That night, lying awake on a fold-out bed in his grandparents' living room, Dwayne thought hard about all the successful men he admired – Sylvester Stallone, Bruce Willis and Arnold Schwarzenegger were three of them, and as he was drifting off to sleep he realized that they all had one thing in common. They were action stars who'd put a lot of time and energy into building their bodies. As young men they'd dedicated hours and hours to keeping fit and lifting weights. They'd received attention for their impressive physiques and used this to develop successful acting careers. Now they were three of the richest and most famous men in the world.

It was a light-bulb moment for Dwayne. Stallone, Willis and Schwarzenegger had made the most of their natural size and strength. Dwayne was big and strong too.

Inspired by his wrestler dad, Dwayne was already working out at the gym. Now, every afternoon, without fail, he began boxing and lifting weights after school.

I figured, maybe, just maybe, training my body would lead me to something big.

Dwayne's hunch was right. It didn't happen right away, but just over a decade later he entered the family business, when he made his World Wrestling Entertainment (WWE) debut and within a few years he was one of the **most successful** wrestlers in WWE history, becoming (in the words of The Rock himself) *'The most electrifying man in all of entertainment.'*

In 2001, Dwayne appeared in his first feature film, *The Mummy Returns*. One role quickly led to another, and by 2019, he'd become the **highest-paid** actor in the whole of Hollywood.

You make it all sound so easy.

Well, from those humble beginnings Dwayne has made an incredible success of his life.

We'll be hearing about the bumps soon enough, but what we really want to know is how he got over them. How did he get where he is today?

1 Dwayne's Rocky Start

Dwayne Douglas Johnson was born on 2nd May 1972 in Hayward, California, and, from the very start, wrestling was a massive part of his life. You could even say it was **in his blood**. After all, Dwayne's dad was a professional wrestler, his grandfather (his mum's dad) was too, and so were two of his uncles and TEN of his cousins. Even his grandmother worked as a wrestling promoter (one of the first female promoters in wrestling history); at one point she was overseeing the entire Polynesian Pro Wrestling circuit! So, it's fair to say, young Dwayne lived and breathed wrestling too.

Professional wrestling became popular in the 1920s. In the 1940s each of the three major US TV stations aired wrestling shows and every week millions of Americans tuned in to watch. But by the late 1950s, audiences were losing interest and ratings plummeted.

My dad was my hero, but he didn't have it easy. He was called Rocky Johnson, and things were pretty tough for wrestlers when he came on the scene.

Rocky was a black Canadian from Nova Scotia. He'd had a hard life. His dad had died when he was just 13, and after knocking his mum's violent boyfriend out with a shovel, Rocky had been **forced to leave home** at 14. It was lucky he had a talent as a tag-team wrestler.

TAG TEAMS EXPLAINED

Tag-team wrestlers usually wrestle in teams of two or more, taking it in turns to enter the ring. One team member can't enter the ring until the other tags or touches hands with them on leaving.

Rocky was known to have one of the very best drop kicks

in the business, and with his partner, Tony Atlas, he was breaking new ground too. As 'The Soul Patrol' they were the first ever black tag-team champions in WWE history.

WELCOME TO THE FAMILY

Before Dwayne's parents had even met, Rocky faced his future father-in-law Peter Maivia (Dwayne's grandfather) in the ring. This was the early 1970s, the days before big televised matches and million-dollar salaries, and even though they were both well-respected performers, Rocky and Peter **didn't expect to make much money** from their sport. On the other hand, they couldn't imagine doing anything else with their lives.

Heavily tattooed and built like a rhino, Peter was well known on the wrestling circuit. He'd won championships in the South Pacific and in Hawaii and had moved his family to the USA from American Samoa in the 1970s where he'd added some impressive titles to his name, including heavyweight champion of Texas and US tag-team champion. He was a big cheese back home in American Samoa too. As **high chief** he was expected to look out for his entire extended family (which included hundreds of people!) – protecting their land, settling their disputes and generally leading by good example.

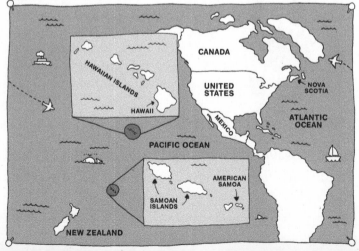

Wrestling is massively popular in Samoa. In fact, most of the wrestlers in Dwayne's family were on his mum's side and originally came from there. Samoans are often tall, wide and very strong – perfectly built for wrestling, basically!

Rocky and Peter **looked ferocious** in the ring, but out of the spotlight, things were rather different. Peter was worried when he found out Rocky didn't have anywhere to stay for the night after the match, so without thinking twice, he said:

Come and stay at my place.

It was a decision Grandpa came to regret!

The moment Rocky set eyes on Peter's only daughter, Ata, **he was smitten**. Ata wasn't quite so sure at first. She could see that Rocky was a good-looking guy, but he chewed tobacco, and she thought that was gross. Rocky was a charmer, though, and it wasn't long before Ata fell madly in love with him. She even got over the tobacco chewing.

Peter wasn't at all happy about the blossoming romance. He knew better than anyone how difficult life on the circuit could be. It was hard enough for the wrestlers, but their wives and girlfriends were often stuck at home for months on end while their husbands and boyfriends were on the road. Peter and his wife, Lia, wanted something better for their daughter, so they came to a decision: Rocky and Ata's relationship **had to stop**.

It was too late, though, Rocky and Ata were already deeply involved. They got together anyway and hoped Peter and Lia would come round once they got used to the idea. It took about a year, but in the end Peter and Lia did give Rocky and Ata their blessing, just in time for another big announcement – a baby.

I brought my family together.

Rocky and Ata never regretted getting together, but Peter and Lia were right: **life was tough from the start**.

Rocky was constantly on the road, performing in shows across the country, and his young family travelled with him whenever they could. By the time Dwayne was at nursery school, he'd already lived in five different states. To young Dwayne, moving around seemed like fun, and watching his dad in the ring was so exciting!

Rocky was a massive hit with the crowd, winning fans wherever he went. Dwayne liked nothing more than sitting with a carton of popcorn on his lap, surrounded by cheering supporters, while his dad performed in the ring.

That's my dad, he'd think proudly.

On Rocky's days off, while most fathers took their kids to the playground, **Rocky took Dwayne to the gym**, though he wasn't allowed to join in until he was a teenager. Instead, he got to sit and watch his dad working out, carefully noting all his best moves.

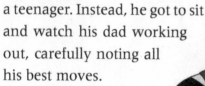

I learned at a very young age that there's no substitute for hard work.

Back at home Dwayne would practise drop kicks and headlocks on the long-suffering family dog for **hours on end**.

Around the age of eight, Dwayne's parents bought him a video camera to keep him occupied when they were busy working. On Friday nights, with the apartment all to himself, Dwayne would set the camera up in the corner and pretend the living room was his very own WWE arena. He imitated everyone, from legendary commentator Vince McMahon, to his three absolute favourite wrestlers – Roddy Piper, Ric Flair and Magnificent Muraco.

WWE Personalities Explained

WWE is as much about the characters as it is about the actual wrestling. It's not enough to be big and strong and win matches – you have to show your personality too.

Wrestlers often start by picking a name that sums up who they are:

The Undertaker

Macho Man

They need to make a grand entrance to grab the audience's attention. Music, special effects and a flashy costume all add to the impact.

Dwayne's dad was a good guy, in the business they'd call him a 'babyface', but Dwayne's favourite wrestlers were all 'heels' – bad guys. They shouted and scowled and got booed by the crowds, but heels had way more fun. And they all had a talent for trash-talk – insulting other players and boasting about themselves.

Roddy Piper – aka Rowdy Roddy, or Hot Rod – was a big-name WWE wrestler in the 1980s and 1990s. Witty, but with a fiery temper, Roddy was Canadian and had Scottish roots. He'd arrive in the ring in his kilt with an escort of Scottish pipes and drums. He shaved the head of one opponent and smashed a coconut over the head of another!

Ric Flair – aka 'The Nature Boy' was a 16-time WWE champion and possibly the greatest wrestler of all time. Fans loved his flamboyant personality and even more flamboyant outfits. With his deep tan and white-blond hair, he'd arrive in OTT robes, sometimes gold, sometimes trimmed with feathers, and massively expensive shoes.

Magnificent Muraco (real name Donald) was the villain fans loved to hate back in the 80s because he seemed so arrogant, taking absolutely no notice of the rules. Audiences often tried to put him off, but they hardly ever succeeded. Muraco was not only the Intercontinental Champion twice (that's the most important title in the whole of the WWE), but he managed to hold on to the title longer than nearly anyone else in WWE history.

Attitude Problem

Believe it or not, Dwayne was a **scrawny** baby, but he soon grew to be big and strong. Although he liked wrestling a lot, he didn't really think about becoming a professional wrestler himself when he was young, and his family definitely didn't encourage him. In fact, they did everything they could to steer him towards a more sensible career.

As Dwayne entered his teens, the novelty of moving around all the time had worn off. After a brief stint in New Zealand, the family had settled in Hawaii for a while, where his grandparents were living. It was nice to stay in one place for a bit, but money was as scarce as ever and school was tough for a kid who was big for his age and had a pretty famous dad.

One day, Dwayne was set upon by a group of **25 older boys**. He was lucky to escape with just a few scratches and bruises. When Rocky found out what had happened, he was furious and insisted on coming to school to confront the bullies. Once the boys saw Dwayne's championship wrestler dad face to face, they were terrified. They left Dwayne alone after that, but there was plenty more trouble to come.

Rocky was often away in Nashville, USA, while Ata worked all hours cleaning hotel rooms to cover the weekly rent of $120.

It was a struggle, and Dwayne wasn't helping. He wasn't exactly the model student, often disrupting class or skipping lessons altogether. Then he started getting into trouble on a regular basis. When he bothered to go to school, he still had fights with the other kids. Outside school, he fell in with a gang of boys who targeted rich tourists, stealing their money and jewellery. Dwayne was **arrested several times** and very nearly ended up inside a juvenile prison. His parents tried to shield him as best they could, but they worried he really would end up in prison one day. Dwayne needed a change of scene and, partly thanks to the eviction notice, one finally came.

When the news reached Dwayne that the family were on the move yet again, he didn't mind too much. He loved Hawaii and being so close to his grandparents, but he could see it was time for a fresh start.

The New Kid

After a few short stints at other schools in Tennessee, Dwayne arrived at Freedom High School in the small city of Bethlehem, Pennsylvania, with a dodgy pencil moustache and a chip on his shoulder. He'd been a pretty skinny kid, but as a teenager he suddenly went through a **massive growth spurt**. Thanks to his Samoan heritage, his shape had changed and at only 15 years old, he was already approaching a whopping 193 cm (6 foot 4 inches) tall and weighed in at roughly 100 kg (16 stone). He **towered over** most of his classmates, and it wasn't long before rumours were flying that he wasn't a student at all . . .

Dwayne's first year at Bethlehem was hard. The undercover cop stuff eventually died down, but Dwayne's classmates still weren't exactly friendly. You'd think other students would have avoided picking fights with him, but for some reason, Dwayne became a target for kids who wanted to show off how tough they were.

Inspired by his dad's punishing workout routine (getting up at 5 a.m. every day to lift weights), Dwayne had started working out when he was 13. Now he was hitting the gym almost every day before or after school. So, when he overheard a rumour that he was taking steroids, **Dwayne got mad**.

How could anyone think he'd taken drugs when he'd been putting in so much effort at the gym! He couldn't let it go, and he made it his mission to track down the kid who'd started the rumour.

One morning at break, he spotted the boy in question walking down the corridor and confronted him. The boy refused to apologize, and Dwayne began to raise his voice. They started arguing, one thing led to another and the boy pushed Dwayne. No way could Dwayne let that go, so he returned the push. Unfortunately, he pushed a bit too much – the boy fell backwards and hit his head so hard he was **knocked unconscious**.

Dwayne was horrified by what had happened, but it was too late to make amends – the damage was done. He was promptly suspended for three days and spent the rest of the school year struggling to shake off his reputation as a **troublemaker**.

He hadn't meant to hurt the boy, but there was no denying that Dwayne had a temper and an attitude that often didn't do him any favours.

One day, Dwayne decided he didn't want to use the boys' toilets. They did smell **disgusting**, to be fair. Instead, he swaggered into the teachers' lounge and used their facilities. He was casually washing his hands when a gruff voice behind him said, 'Hey, you can't be in here.' Dwayne cast a glance over his shoulder and saw the school's head football coach, Jody Cwik, standing behind him. It was clear he wasn't impressed. Still, Dwayne just continued with what he was doing, saying:

Dwayne finished washing his hands, dried them on a towel and left the room. Jody hadn't said another word, but Dwayne could tell he was angry.

In Samoan culture, *alofa* (love) and *fa'aaloalo* (respect) are hugely important, especially when it comes to the treatment of your elders. That night **Dwayne could barely sleep** for thinking how rude and disrespectful he'd been to Jody. He only managed to drop off to sleep after he'd made the firm decision to make amends.

The following day, he entered the teachers' lounge again, this time to apologize to Jody for the way he'd behaved. Fully expecting a good telling-off, Dwayne wasn't quite prepared for Jody's response. The coach accepted the apology, shook Dwayne's hand and asked him for a favour . . .

Dwayne quickly agreed, figuring it was the least he could do.

He'd played football back in Hawaii and enjoyed it well enough; he just hadn't ever thought about taking it any further. All that changed at Bethlehem High School.

DWAYNE HITS THE FOOTBALL FIELD

Jody was one of the first teachers to really take notice of Dwayne and spot his potential. In return, Dwayne put his all into playing football.

Unfortunately, Bethlehem High School's team was **pretty terrible**! Despite Jody's best efforts, they lost more games than they won. Even so, Dwayne soon realized he enjoyed playing, whatever the result. In fact, losing regularly gave Dwayne the time and space to really analyse the game and work on his individual skills. His attention to detail paid off. He became **team captain** and was even made All American.

Being made 'All American' is a pretty big honour. It's a title given to high-school and college athletes who are considered to be outstanding in their chosen sport.

1989 marked Dwayne's final year at high school. Up to this point, he'd kind of assumed he might end up following in his dad's footsteps and becoming a wrestler (though the family were still dead against it).

But then he started getting recruitment letters from colleges across the country.

In the USA, college football is big business, attracting big crowds and bringing in essential funds for the colleges. So any college with a strong football programme is keen to get their hands on the very best players from high schools across the country. It seemed Dwayne Johnson was one of the players on their radar.

HOME   AWAY

THE NATIONAL FOOTBALL LEAGUE EXPLAINED

College football programmes are the training grounds for anyone hoping to play for the National Football League (NFL): America's professional football league. And anyone who plays for the NFL is basically set for life.

The NFL has been around for over a hundred years and, these days, consists of 32 teams. The season actually lasts just 17 weeks between September and December each year, building up to a final game – the Super Bowl – to decide that year's winning team.

The Super Bowl is one of the biggest and most-watched club sporting events in the world. I never miss it, even though my favourite NFL team, the Miami Dolphins, haven't won the title since 1973!

It was an exciting time. Pretty much overnight, any thoughts of becoming a wrestler went out of the window and, as the days went on, Dwayne found himself **bombarded with offers** of scholarships from all sorts of colleges. Some sent letters. Others called him.

You won't regret coming to Florida State University!

Dear Dwayne,
Have we got the opportunity for you . . .

Some even turned up on his doorstep or caught him on the way home from school.

A few colleges even offered him extra financial incentives on top of the scholarship (which would cover Dwayne's tuition fees and basic living expenses). Several promised Dwayne that he would be 'very well taken care of' if he chose their college – a common tactic used to lure the very best high-school players from across the country.

Dwayne was extremely flattered, of course, not to mention tempted, since his family didn't have a lot of money, but he was only really interested in one college. Dwayne was desperate for a place at the University of Miami, home of the legendary Hurricanes.

Over five seasons, under head coach Jimmy Johnson, the Hurricanes had won a staggering **50 games out of 60** (playing against other college teams from all over the country), including a national championship in 1987. Sadly, Jimmy had already moved on to coach the Dallas Cowboys, but Miami still had one of the best football programmes in the country. As well as being great on the field, the Hurricanes were well known for being cocky, full of swagger and masters of trash-talk (just like Dwayne's favourite WWE heels).

Another attraction was the weather. Having spent the last few years in chilly Pennsylvania, Dwayne missed the year-round Hawaiian sunshine. He wanted to go to college somewhere warm and sunny and Miami definitely fitted the bill – it's in the Sunshine State: Florida. Yep, all things considered, Dwayne felt pretty certain the University of Miami was the place for him.

The problem was, he hadn't heard a peep from them.

'Why don't you just pick one of the other colleges?' his mum said, but Dwayne had a feeling he just couldn't shake that **his destiny was to be a Hurricane**.

So, he decided, if the University of Miami wasn't going to contact him, he'd just have to take matters into his own hands. Bold as you like, he called the college and spoke to one of the Hurricanes' coaches, Bob Karmelowicz (aka Coach Karm).

It turned out that Dwayne's name was on their list of possible recruits, but for some reason it had slipped through the cracks. Impressed with Dwayne's enthusiasm, Coach Karm agreed to come and meet him.

Coach Karm was nothing like the other coaches Dwayne had met. He made **no promises** and didn't give incentives. Instead he told Dwayne:

Dwayne loved Coach Karm's straight-talking attitude. The other recruiters had struck Dwayne as somehow dishonest. He agreed to take the place then and there.

He wasn't bothered about the money or the perks. He was going to be a Hurricane and that was all that mattered.

2   HURRICANE DWAYNE

Dwayne moved to Miami in early August 1990 and hit the ground running. He got stuck into pre-season practice right away.

Back at Bethlehem High School, Dwayne had been a pretty big fish in a small pond – the captain of the team and its biggest, strongest player. At Miami, he was just one member of a team that boasted **over 90 players**, all competing for a place in an 11-a-side game. You might find this hard to believe, but while Dwayne was six foot five by the age of 18, plenty of his Miami team-mates were far taller, and some were quite a few years older too. It was intimidating, but Dwayne was determined not to get spooked. Instead, he used the competition to motivate himself to work even harder.

The Hurricanes' motto was 'All it takes is all you've got!' and Dwayne applied it to everything he did from the moment he arrived on campus. The code of conduct for student athletes was strict. Under the old head coach, the Hurricanes had developed a reputation for bending the rules, with players breezing through their degrees, sometimes without even setting foot in a classroom. New head coach, Dennis Erickson, was determined to clean up the team's image. Under his watch, all players would be required to put in an effort both on and off the field if they didn't want to be thrown out.

Practice was full on from the start. As well as time on the field, all players had to do sessions in the weights room every day. **The atmosphere was hugely competitive** – every player wanted one of the 11 starting positions on the team.

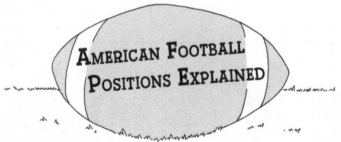

AMERICAN FOOTBALL POSITIONS EXPLAINED

In American football, players tend to stick to one position. The coach then selects which players to use based on whether the team are playing 'offense' – with the ball – or 'defense' – trying to prevent the offense from scoring. The teams face each other at the scrimmage line, with the football in between them.

NFL Positions

OFFENSIVE

Running back: runs with the ball; can catch short passes.

Fullback: block for the running back and quarterback; can run with the ball.

Quarterback: leads the team. Gets the ball at the start of play and guides it down the field.

Wide receiver: speeds past the other team's defenders and aims to catch the ball.

Tight end: receives passes and protects the quarterback.

Tackle: tries to block the fastest opponents; protects the quarterback.

Guard: protects the quarterback and ball carriers.

Centre: passes (snaps) the ball back to the quarterback at the start of play. Handles the ball on every play.

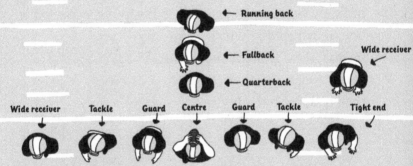

'Line of scrimmage' between the two sides

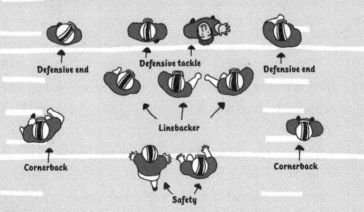

DEFENSIVE

Safety: defends the deep pass.

Cornerback: lines up on the wide parts of the field, usually marking the offensive receivers.

Linebacker: tackles and defends against players running with or passing the ball.

Defensive end: tackles the quarterback or ball carrier.

Defensive tackle: tackles and prevents the other team from running with the ball.

Only 11 players from each team can be on the field at any one time during a game, but Dwayne had to compete with **up to seven or eight** other guys, all vying for the same position. Each day a 'depth chart' was posted on the wall of the locker room, rating the players from best to worst. Dwayne's position was defensive tackle. As a freshman (first-year student) it was highly unlikely he'd get to play. Most freshmen expected to be 'redshirted', which basically means they practise with the team and wear their kit on match days, but only get a game as a last resort.

If Jason was sick, Pedro was injured and Alex got booked, I might get to play!

Dwayne wasn't very experienced, but he threw himself into practice, doing everything at full speed and with maximum effort, hoping he'd make his mark early on. Good technique could come later, he told himself, he just **had to get himself noticed**.

A few weeks in, he checked the depth chart and there was his name listed with seven others under the defensive tackle position. But he was at number two! The team's star player, Russell Maryland, would start the game but Dwayne would be the first choice if it came to a substitution. Dwayne was higher on the chart than guys who were older and more experienced than him and the season hadn't even started yet.

It was only a matter of time before that number-one defensive tackle spot was mine.

A SPANNER IN THE WORKS

Things were moving along nicely when, just 10 days before the first game of the season, **disaster struck**. In the middle of a practice session Dwayne was suddenly slammed to the ground from behind. He felt a searing pain in his shoulder and let out an anguished howl. He didn't need to look to know what had just happened – he'd felt his shoulder pop right out of its socket!

One of the medics managed to pop it back in again, but the damage was done. An MRI scan revealed that Dwayne had a separated shoulder and torn ligaments. The good news was that, with surgery, he'd make a full recovery. The bad news? **He'd need to take the entire season off**. Dwayne was devastated, but if he was going to realize his dream of playing professional football, this was the only way. With a heavy heart, he agreed to the surgery.

Pretty much overnight, Dwayne went from being number-two defensive tackle to the **least important** member of the team, and he hated it. He hadn't realized just how much he'd been enjoying himself until everything was taken away from him. Adjusting to life as an injured player was a struggle. He was still encouraged to come to team meetings and watch the games, but being around his fit and able team-mates was just too painful. After a while, he stopped turning up. He spent a lot of time hiding miserably in his room, or on the payphone to his parents, trying his best not to let on he was crying.

No, honest, Mom, I'm absolutely fine!

You'd think Dwayne might have distracted himself by putting all his energy into his college work, but instead he started skipping classes and **staying in bed all day**, feeling seriously sorry for himself.

In December, Coach Karm called Dwayne in to his office. The coach sounded stern, but Dwayne wasn't too worried, expecting another of Karm's harmless peptalks. It was only when Dwayne saw the piece of paper on the coach's desk that he started to feel a little nervous. It was his college report card.

Dwayne didn't need to look to know **his grades weren't great**. Hardly surprising, really, as he'd skipped more than half his classes and hadn't even bothered turning up to a couple of exams. Still, he didn't panic. He may have been injured, but he was a Hurricane; Coach Karm would sort him out. Everything would be OK.

A WAKE-UP CALL

But things were far from OK. Coach Karm was really angry. He started ranting and raving. Dwayne left his office fully aware that he'd disappointed the coach, the college, his parents, not to mention himself. He thought about catching the first bus out of town, **waving goodbye** to college and football for ever, but after he'd calmed down a little, he realized how stupid that would be. There was no point throwing everything away.

I knew I had to stop feeling sorry for myself. I'd been determined to succeed. It was up to me to fix this situation.

From then on, Dwayne was expected to do an extra two hours of supervised study each day, go to weekly meetings with a tutor and get a tutor's signature after each lecture or class, to prove to Coach Karm that he'd been there. If he missed a single class, he could forget football training that day.

It was all so **humiliating**. College football players had a reputation for being lazy or stupid (or both), and Dwayne felt like he was living proof that it was true.

Things were tough on his parents back home too. Rocky's wrestling career was coming to an end. It was every wrestler's biggest fear, and Rocky hadn't thought about it carefully enough. With no back-up plan, money was tighter than ever. Rocky hadn't had much of an education, so he was forced to take a truck-driving job. It was a **big comedown** for a one-time champion, and it was hard for Dwayne to see his hero dad having to settle into ordinary life. This might have helped Dwayne decide to turn that corner . . . or maybe it was something, or someone, else . . .

3   DWAYNE FALLS HARD

Dwayne had always been popular with girls. He'd even managed to take **two different dates** to his high-school prom without either of them catching on!

As a member of the Hurricanes, even with his injury, it was easy to catch the eye of a female student. Dwayne was happily carrying on his old ways, but then **he met someone special** . . .

He was in a bar with some friends one evening, when he felt someone elbow him in his side. He whirled round to discover a girl looking up at him – a very pretty girl with dark hair, big brown eyes and a killer smile.

She held out her hand for Dwayne to shake.

Hi, I've seen you in the weights room. I'm Dany.

Dwayne was seriously impressed. Dany wasn't just beautiful, she was smart (a senior, studying International Finance and Marketing), sporty (a member of the university rowing team) and full of confidence. But he didn't want to let on just how keen he was, at least not straight away. When Dany asked him to dance, he said he couldn't hit the dance floor until a certain song came on.

'Um, OK then,' Dany said, assuming he wasn't interested and walking away.

The second she turned her back Dwayne was desperate to talk to her some more. A few minutes later, a song called 'Groove is in the Heart' began to play. Dwayne ran over to Dany's table and pulled her up to dance. By the end of the song, **he had fallen for her big time**.

Dany was crazy about Dwayne too, even though

she was four years older than him – she was 22 while he was still just 18. Unfortunately, **her parents weren't impressed**. History was about to repeat itself.

Just as Peter and Lia Maivia had disapproved of Rocky getting together with their daughter, Dany's parents were dead set against Dany dating Dwayne. As well as the age gap, they thought Dwayne's dream of playing for the NFL was just pie in the sky. What if he didn't get picked for a professional team? What would he do with his life then? Whatever the answer to that question, in her parents' eyes, Dwayne was nowhere near good enough for their Dany.

They hadn't even met me!

So, just as Rocky and Ata had done before them, Dany and Dwayne carried on seeing each other against her parents' wishes. But now, Dwayne was working harder than ever, in the classroom and on the pitch. After a few months off, he'd recovered from his injury and was **full of determination**: to prove himself on the football field, find a way to support his parents, and to one day prove Dany's parents wrong.

Standing Out For All The Wrong Reasons

Being around so many talented footballers all the time, Dwayne started to realize that he wasn't necessarily the most naturally talented performer on the field. However, what he lacked in natural ability, he made up for with strength, determination and versatility. Above all else, **he was a grafter** and going into his second (sophomore) year, he hoped this might be enough to help him make a career from football.

His efforts seemed to be paying off in the classroom – he even got a few As! – but no matter how hard he worked on the football field, it was getting more and more difficult to stand out from the other players.

While Dwayne had been recovering, the other guys had made good progress, and the competition for the number-one defensive tackle spot was tougher than ever. It was great that he was getting to play, but Dwayne was never picked to be on the pitch from the beginning of the game as a starter, and that was frustrating him.

The pressure, the effort he was putting in, the struggle for his parents and his difficulties impressing Dany's parents all came to a head one day in the weights room office. A fellow Hurricane, Kevin, made a joke about Dwayne's performance that day in practice. Dwayne took it the wrong way. Moments later they were trading insults across the desk, and the next thing anyone knew **the office was trashed**.

So embarrassing. We had to be separated by the rest of the team.

It wasn't the only time Dwayne lost his cool. A few weeks later he did it again – only this time he had a much bigger audience. At an away game against San Diego State University, a fight broke out between the players. Dwayne didn't need much of an invitation to join in and ended up chasing their mascot halfway across the football field.

I'll kill you! I'll kill you!

Unfortunately, the game was being screened on national television, and that night Dwayne's antics were featured on **every sporting highlights show** on TV!

His mother was furious. She phoned him to tell him off for behaving so childishly. Once he'd calmed down, Dwayne realized that she was right; he'd made a complete fool of himself. He'd always had a temper, but losing it front of so many people (not to mention his coaches) was a massive turning point. He did his best to apologize and made a secret vow to do everything he could to keep his emotions in check in future.

In the spring of Dwayne's junior (third) year, Dwayne and Dany made the decision to move in together. Dany's parents were furious when she told them. Without even asking to meet Dwayne, they gave her an ultimatum: it was them or Dwayne. **Dany chose Dwayne**.

It was a painful time, but Dany's decision showed Dwayne she had total faith in him.

I was more determined to succeed than ever. I had to prove to Dany (and her parents) that I was worth the risk.

Disaster Strikes Again

Dwayne kept putting in the maximum effort on the football field and he felt his performance was OK. He got lots of playing time, felt like he'd made a good contribution to the team and had high hopes for his final, senior, year. Suddenly, his dream of playing for the NFL didn't seem all that crazy after all. He just needed to keep doing what he was doing.

Then, one day in his senior year, **everything went wrong**. In the middle of a 'bull rush' drill (where defensive linemen push their opponents backwards) he felt a sharp pain shoot down his lower back and through his legs.

He completed the training session but knew something wasn't right. After a bunch of tests, he found out he'd ruptured a couple of discs in his spine. Dwayne was forced to admit that his injury was so serious, he **might never play football again**. The doctor told him to rest completely for two weeks, but it was only about two days before he hit the weights room.

Dwayne ignored the advice and carried on for the rest of the season, trying to block out the pain, but sometimes it was so intense, his team-mates had to help him get in and out of his kit. After one particularly uncomfortable game in Pittsburgh, Dwayne couldn't even sit in his seat on the plane ride home. He had to lie on the floor at the back, while the cabin crew stepped over him!

Don't mind me.

Dwayne finally took a two-week break and managed to get through the last few weeks of the football season. No matter how determined he was, though, it was becoming obvious that other members of the team were outshining him. Hard work alone simply wasn't going to be enough to get to the top.

The annual NFL Scouting Combine – where college players undergo tests in front of NFL coaches, managers and scouts – happened in February 1995 and **Dwayne wasn't even invited**. He might still get an NFL contract, but his chances weren't great, and he felt snubbed nonetheless. Still, he wasn't ready to give up on his dream quite yet, so he signed with a sports agent based in Los Angeles, hoping to find an alternative route to a place with an NFL team.

A Lifeline?

Dwayne sat by the phone and waited for it to ring. It didn't. He refused to give up hope; a team might still pick him up before the new football season began.

Any minute now . . .

The months crept by. Dwayne graduated from the University of Miami with a degree in General Studies (specializing in criminology and physiology) but no footballing job. Meanwhile, a number of his team-mates were all set to start their professional careers. It was looking like this dream was never going to happen. He was just starting to face some uncomfortable facts when **the phone finally rang**!

His agent had got him a football job. Yesss! There was one tiny catch . . .

It was miles away . . . in Canada!

4   DWAYNE HITS ROCK BOTTOM

Even if it meant living apart from Dany, for Dwayne this was a no-brainer. He'd been disappointed and frustrated over the last few years, but he still wanted to play professional football and he only had one offer on the table. **He had no option but to take it**. Dwayne would be joining the Calgary Stampeders, part of the West Division of the Canadian Football League (the CFL).

Training in Calgary began in the summer of 1995 and things didn't go too smoothly. Canadian football rules restrict the number of non-Canadian players in a team. As there were already two other American players up for the defensive tackle position, it soon became clear that there wouldn't be room for all three of them on Calgary Stampeders' roster.

Wally Buono, the team's head coach, told Dwayne he didn't have a place on the main team. He had a choice, Wally explained apologetically: go home and try again next season, or stay and train with the practice team until a permanent spot opened up. Dwayne chose to stay. At least that way he'd be playing football and getting paid for it.

Unfortunately, the wage for a practice player was **pretty abysmal**. Once Dwayne had paid commission to his agent, he was left with about $175 per week to pay for food, rent, bills and anything else he needed. It just wasn't enough. He moved into a cramped and grubby unfurnished apartment with three other practice players who were all in the same boat.

With no furniture and no money, they slept on **dirty old mattresses** they found round the back of an old motel and used upturned crates as tables and chairs. They ate nothing but pasta and cheap spaghetti sauce and told each other stupid jokes to keep their spirits up.

Dwayne didn't even have that much to do. As a member of the practice team, he only had to train four days a week, and he suddenly found himself with a lot of time on his hands. He'd head to the stadium, even on the days he wasn't needed, just to keep himself busy.

Even practice team players got free tickets to the Stampeders' home games, but Dwayne generally sold his outside the stadium for cash. He'd watch the game on TV.

Finally, after he'd been in Calgary for two months, a call came from his agent to say the team was **letting him go** altogether.

My football career was over before it had even begun.

Dwayne couldn't bear to stay in Calgary a moment longer. The following morning, he said goodbye to his roommates and headed straight for the airport.

Arriving in Miami late that night he was feeling thoroughly miserable. He sat down on a bench and turned out his pockets.

He had exactly **seven dollars** to his name.

At the age of 23, Dwayne felt like he had finally **hit rock bottom**. He had no money, no car, no career, and what felt like no future.

Back at his apartment in Miami, he and Dany talked into the night about what he should do next. He'd spent hours at a time daydreaming while he'd been in Calgary, and he'd realized something. He hadn't been daydreaming so much about playing for the NFL; his mind had been wandering back to the world of wrestling. When he told Dany . . .

Forget football. I want to move back with my folks and train to be a wrestler.

. . . it was a **huge bombshell**. He was fully prepared for her to tell him the idea was crazy but, to her credit, she was actually really supportive. She told him she would be behind him whatever he wanted to do.

Dwayne didn't need telling twice. He dashed straight to the nearest payphone (this was the 1990s, remember, so hardly anyone owned a mobile) and called his parents.

Rocky answered.

'Dad, it's Dwayne. I'm in Miami. Can you come pick me up?'

A New Direction

The drive to Tampa, Florida, where his parents lived, was long and pretty uncomfortable. Dwayne revealed his plan to train to be a wrestler early in the journey, and Rocky's response **wasn't exactly enthusiastic**. He reminded Dwayne how physically demanding wrestling was, how no performer could keep it up for ever, that non-stop travel was part and parcel of the job . . . Wrestling was just as hard as football, Rocky reckoned, if not harder. And there was another problem. Dwayne had never even been in a wrestling ring.

The argument didn't stop there. Every night for the following week, Dwayne and Rocky had a variation of the same heated conversation – Dwayne begging Rocky to train him to be a wrestler and Rocky doing his very best to talk him out of it. Eventually Dwayne tried a different approach.

'Fine,' he said. 'If you won't train me, I'll find someone else who will.'

This did the trick. If his son was really going to give wrestling a try, Rocky wanted to be the one to get him up to speed.

'OK,' he agreed. 'I'll teach you the basics. Just be prepared to **work harder than you've ever worked in your life**.'

Dwayne wasn't worried. He already knew all about hard work! He shook his dad's hand and the deal was done.

5   DWAYNE IN THE RING

Dwayne's very first training session happened the following week. Rocky was busy working so he got his good friend Ron Slinker, a one-time professional wrestler and martial artist, to put Dwayne through his paces.

Ron started with the basics – walking and locking up (when wrestlers grapple with each other at the beginning of a match). Dwayne took to it right away. He'd never felt like he was a complete natural on the football field, but **wrestling made complete sense** to him from the very start. That had to be a good sign.

At one point during the session, Dwayne caught sight of himself in the mirror and liked what he saw. After years of crushing disappointment and setbacks, he finally felt like he was on the right path.

After two hours they finished training, and almost every muscle in his body ached. Not that Dwayne cared – he was on such a high, he barely even noticed the pain.

At his next session, Rocky was in charge and they moved on from the basics to headlocks, hammerlocks and spots. It was a lot to take in, but **Dwayne loved every second**.

Headlock: An upper-body throw where you grab your opponent's head and arm and toss them over your hip.

Hammerlock: A hold in which one arm of an opponent is twisted and forced upwards behind his back.

Spot: A move or series of moves.

GRIND HARD, SHINE HARD

From that moment on, **Dwayne was hooked**. He got a job as a personal trainer to make ends meet and spent the rest of his time training himself, getting up at six o'clock every morning and heading straight to the gym. He carried a notebook everywhere he went and was constantly scribbling down ideas for moves. He ate, slept and even dreamed wrestling.

There was one thing that was challenging him, though. Dwayne knew he needed to come up with a wrestling name, he just didn't have a clue where to start. He definitely didn't want to link himself with his dad or granddad, because he wanted to build his own reputation and **stand on his own two feet**. So, when his mum and dad suggested . . .

. . . Dwayne wasn't impressed.

He was still trying to decide on his name when he got the news he'd been waiting for. Pat Patterson, a big cheese at the WWE (World Wrestling Entertainment) and an old wrestling friend of his dad's, had agreed to come and meet Dwayne at the gym that weekend.

Today, the WWE is the biggest wrestling promotion in the world, screening wrestling matches to millions of fans in 135 countries, but back in the 1960s and 1970s (when Rocky was wrestling for them), it was nowhere near as popular or well known.

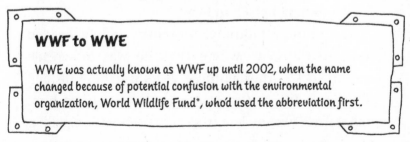

WWF to WWE

WWE was actually known as WWF up until 2002, when the name changed because of potential confusion with the environmental organization, World Wildlife Fund*, who'd used the abbreviation first.

*It's called the World Wide Fund for Nature in the UK.

Then, in the 1980s, thanks to huge personalities, like Hulk Hogan, wrestling enjoyed a massive boost, and by the time Dwayne expressed an interest, it was a multi-million-dollar industry. He knew if he wanted to make it as a wrestler, he needed to get on their main roster, and impressing Pat would be the perfect way to start. But Pat hadn't seen Dwayne since he was 14 years old . . .

My, you've grown!

It was going to be a big weekend. On top of Pat's visit, Dany was also coming to stay. She'd never seen Dwayne wrestle before, and she was excited about watching him in the ring, but she had **no idea** what she was letting herself in for!

On Saturday morning, the entire family headed down to the gym, where Dwayne was to wrestle against Rocky. After all those years watching his dad perform, it felt pretty strange to be up against him, and at first Dwayne had to stop himself from giggling.

Luckily, the second the match began, father and son had forgotten about their relationship and put on their very best game faces.

Unfortunately, Dwayne hadn't explained to Dany that most of his groans and grimaces were just for show; he wasn't really hurt (it's known as 'selling' in the wrestling business). At one point, Dwayne hit the mat so hard **the entire ring shook**! He really went to town, moaning, writhing and clutching his back. Dany, who knew all about Dwayne's history of back injuries, was so horrified she called out:

At that point, Dwayne couldn't help himself. He did something extremely unprofessional. He **stopped the match** to let Dany know he was OK. The other wrestlers in the gym were appalled, but Dwayne felt terrible that Dany was so upset! He was kind of excited too. Dany knew him inside out. If she'd believed that he was really hurt, convincing those big audiences would be a piece of cake.

After the match, Dwayne was keen to know what Pat thought.

'You're going to be OK,' Pat told him, patting him on the back.

It might not sound like a ringing endorsement, but Dwayne was thrilled. Pat was a straight talker. If he'd thought Dwayne had no chance in the business, he would have said so.

Dwayne's instincts were right. A week later, Pat called with fantastic news. Vince McMahon, founder and owner of the WWE wanted to see him in action.

Dwayne was so excited he nearly dropped the phone.

'When? Where?' he asked.

'Corpus Christi, Texas,' came the reply.

Dwayne couldn't believe it. A real match in a real stadium!

There was just one small problem – he still **didn't have a name**.

'FLEXING' SOME MUSCLE

Dwayne didn't have any proper wrestling gear either. A lot of wrestlers wore costumes or masks or face paint for their matches but none of that appealed to Dwayne. To start with, he wanted to **keep things simple** – just boots and a pair of trunks. With only a few days to prepare for his match and still very short of cash, he was forced to borrow some trunks from Meng, a Polynesian wrestler friend of his grandfather's.

Meng was huge, even more enormous than Dwayne, so most of his trunks were way too big. There was one pair that weren't too baggy. Dwayne borrowed the boots from his dad and bought a pair of white kneepads to complete the look.

Hmm, not bad!

Trunks:
stylish electric purple, several sizes too big

Boots:
two sizes too small

Dwayne was ready to rumble.

The match was due to take place on 10th March 1996. It would be a 'dark match', which meant it would happen before or after an actual televised show, but without the TV cameras – the **perfect opportunity** for WWE bosses to test out new talent in front of a big crowd.

Dwayne would be wrestling a performer called Steve Lombardi, aka the Brooklyn Brawler.

THE BROOKLYN BRAWLER

Steve was a *'low-tier midcarder'* in the WWE, which means he was never a headline act. Instead he filled in when he was needed and rarely got to win. He was a safe pair of hands and particularly skilled at making his opponents look good – the perfect rival for rookie Dwayne.

It was usual procedure for the performers to get together before the match, so Dwayne and Steve headed to the canteen to plan out a routine over lunch.

There are winners and losers in WWE shows, but they aren't proper sporting contests. The real focus is on entertainment, with the matches featuring characters, storylines and scripts. And while it all looks spontaneous, **every move is carefully planned**. Any surprise wins are carefully planned too; the organizers of the matches **choose the winners in advance** so the wrestlers always know the outcome before they enter the ring.

The moves themselves are never faked. They really are very physically demanding and can put performers at risk of injury, even death, if they aren't performed correctly. But because the players are following a script, it means they can put all their energy into pulling off a range of ambitious moves.

Steve was hugely experienced and within a short space of time he and Dwayne had an eight-minute routine all planned out.

First I'll do a drop kick, then you can do a body slam . . .

Dwayne wrote it down and spent the next few hours walking through the routine backstage, determined not to put a foot wrong once he was in the ring.

Sharing a dressing room with the other wrestlers – household names like The Undertaker and Bret Hart – it was hard not to be star-struck. It was hard not to feel a bit shabby too in comparison to these seasoned professionals with their extravagant costumes. Still, Dwayne was **absolutely thrilled** to be there.

THE UNDERTAKER

One of the most respected
wrestlers of all time, making
his WWE debut back in 1990.
As the name suggests he
liked a hint of darkness in his

performances, always dressing in black, with a trademark
long leather coat, hat and eye make-up. His run of 21
straight victories at WWE's most famous annual event –
WrestleMania – was so legendary it became known as 'the
streak'.

BRET HART AKA 'THE HITMAN'

Bret came from a wrestling family,
like Dwayne. He wore a 'uniform'
of pink and black and was rarely
seen entering the ring without
his famous mirrored sunglasses.
Hart was a babyface and an ultra-reliable performer who
always put his opponents' safety first. In a world of often
quite cartoonish characters, he focused on the athletic
side of wrestling and worked hard to make his moves look
as slick as possible. His brother Owen was also a popular
WWE wrestler, but sadly he died in 1999 when a stunt
went tragically wrong.

> The accident didn't happen in
> the ring, but wrestling moves
> can be dangerous, even though
> they're carefully planned out.

Before the match, Dwayne found himself a quiet corner, said a short prayer, and headed over to the 'gorilla position', just behind the curtain that divides the players from their audience.

'So, what's your name?' a member of the backstage crew asked Dwayne. 'We need to announce you.'

He'd been racking his brains for weeks, but still failed to come up with anything.

'Um, Dwayne Johnson,' he replied.

The stagehand wasn't impressed, and Dwayne felt embarrassed. He realized if he wanted to be taken seriously, he was going to have to come up with something soon.

Then the music started to play, and it was time. Plain Dwayne strutted out into the ring to the sound of loud jeers. He was a new face, **a complete nobody** as far as the crowd was concerned. He knew he couldn't expect anything less than hostility. Still, it was hard not to feel a bit rattled when the Brooklyn Brawler entered to loud cheers. And it was part of the job not to be thrown by the crowd's reaction. He did his best to block out the noise and concentrate on the routine, hoping all the while that he might change their minds.

There was a lot of pressure. WWE boss Vince McMahon was in the audience, and Dwayne needed to impress him if he was going to have any hope of getting on the main roster.

Although he hid it well, Dwayne **quaked with nerves** as the Brooklyn Brawler made his first move. For a moment, he was worried he might forget everything they'd planned out and miss his chance to impress, but then his focus kicked in and the match went off without a hitch.

The finishing move was a 'small package' (also known as an inside cradle).

It's a fiddly move but thanks to all his preparation, Dwayne pulled it off perfectly, and seconds later he was declared the winner of the match. The audience hadn't been expecting that, but they applauded anyway. It was by no means rapturous, but **Dwayne didn't care.** Any applause sounded better than the booing he'd entered the ring to. What was most exciting was that the WWE bosses had picked him to win the match. It meant they really had faith in him.

Dwayne was in the ring again the next night, pitted against a wrestler called Chris Candido, whose style was completely different from the Brooklyn Brawler's. It was obvious the WWE were testing his versatility, and Dwayne was **determined not to disappoint**. When Chris suggested an advanced move called the Frankensteiner, Dwayne agreed straight away. He didn't tell Chris that he'd never attempted it before.

Trying not to panic, Dwayne spent the hours leading up to the match obsessively practising the move in his head again and again, all the time worrying he might not be able to execute it in real life.

The Frankensteiner was invented by Scott Steiner in the 1980s. It works like this:

It's not a move for the faint of heart!

In the end, much to his relief, the move worked a treat! It didn't win him the match, but he'd known that before he stepped in the ring. Victory belonged to Chris that night, but Dwayne had **put up one heck of a fight**. He was delighted with his performance; the question was, would Vince McMahon and the other head honchos at the WWE agree?

Back in Tampa, Dwayne faced an anxious few days waiting for the WWE's feedback, but when the news came it was good. The WWE wanted to offer him a contract! He wasn't top-level material yet, but they were sending him to Memphis, home of the United States Wrestling Association (USWA) and the perfect training ground for Dwayne. Plenty of up-and-coming wrestlers had learned their craft here, without the WWE TV cameras getting in the way and the massive crowds putting them off.

Dwayne agreed immediately.

He used the money he'd saved up from his job at the gym to buy a car, packed up his stuff, kissed Dany goodbye and headed off to Memphis – over 1,000 km (670 miles) away.

He still hadn't sorted out a wrestling name for himself, so the long journey gave him plenty of thinking time. He was proud of his actual name – Dwayne Johnson – but his WWE name needed to be flashy and memorable.

Finally it hit him.

Flex Kavana! That's it!

Flex suggested muscles (and Dwayne had plenty of those!) and Kavana (a Hawaiian name he liked the sound of) hinted at his Samoan heritage.

It was perfect.

WRESTLER FOR HIRE

Dwayne quickly got stuck in to his new life as a rookie wrestler, but he was only earning around $40 a night, so no way could he afford hotels in the towns where his fights were booked. Instead, he rented a rundown apartment in the centre of Memphis and drove back there every night.

The venues on the USWA circuit were **a million miles away** from the flashy arena in Corpus Christi. Dwayne wrestled in barns (with audiences sitting on bales of hay), at fairs, at carnivals, in car parks . . . Some of the rings were so badly worn there were nails sticking through the boards – wrestlers were afraid to hit the floor!

The crowds could be **wild, drunken and often rather rude**. But Dwayne loved the challenge and the unpredictability of it all – he just hoped it wasn't going to last for ever. With that in mind, he checked in with the WWE head office every week to let them know how he was doing, secretly hoping they'd invite him to join the WWE for real.

To keep himself focused, he set out some goals for the next few years:

He worked the USWA circuit for six months before he finally got the call he'd been waiting for.

Dwayne Johnson — Goals 1996

1. In two years, I want to be the Intercontinental Champion.

2. In four years, I want to be the WWE Champion.

3. In five years, I want to be a millionaire.

The WWE wanted him for a trial fight in Columbus, Ohio, against one of the big stars of the WWE TV shows and all-time hero of Dwayne's, Owen Hart (brother of Bret). The match went well, and Owen was full of praise for Dwayne's skill in the ring, but Pat Patterson wasn't quite so complimentary. He told Dwayne his punches just weren't up to scratch and sent him back to Memphis.

Dwayne was disappointed, of course, but he was grateful for the criticism and made it his mission to ensure his punches became the very **best in the business**. He watched videos of all the top punchers, studying their technique, and then practised in the mirror for hours at a time.

Two weeks later, the WWE called again. This time, they wanted to move Dwayne to Connecticut, home of the WWE's corporate headquarters – and their world-class training facility. Dwayne didn't need asking twice. He wasn't where he wanted to be just yet, but it was a big step in the right direction.

Dwayne Makes His Mark

In Connecticut, with a WWE trainer, Dwayne began to try out increasingly outrageous and risky moves. After two months of hard training, he finally got the news he'd been waiting for:

Madison Square Garden is in the heart of New York City, and it's one of the most famous arenas in the world. It's also huge, with enough space for **tens of thousands** of wrestling fans. Dwayne's granddad had wrestled there back in the 1970s and his dad had too, in the 1980s. Now it was Dwayne's turn. This was where he was going to make his debut. Dwayne could hardly believe it!

He was all set to take part in the Survivor Series – one the biggest televised events in the WWE calendar. It consists of a series of tag-team elimination matches, pitting teams of four or five wrestlers against each other until just one is left.

> Talk about making a splash!

Dwayne might have been in the series, but it seemed 'Flex Kavana' wasn't. The WWE bosses weren't so keen.

> Flex Kavana? What kind of name is that?

> We're calling you Rocky Maivia.

Pushing his dad's and his granddad's names together was exactly what Dwayne had been trying to avoid. He didn't want to trade on his wrestling heritage – but the office insisted, and **Dwayne didn't have much choice**.

He didn't get much of a say in Rocky Maivia's character either. He'd be a good guy – a babyface – expected to smile a lot, not say too much, and hope the crowd liked him anyway. Dwayne had grown up idolizing the bad-guy heels, but he was still **learning the ropes**. While his colleagues could trash-talk all they liked, he'd be concentrating on his moves inside the ring.

Dwayne would be part of a team of eight, and the least experienced of the bunch by far. As the group sat down together to make a plan, Dwayne mostly listened – and took a load of notes. Excited by the routine they'd put together, he called his family and told them to be sure to watch the match on TV that night.

Last Man Standing

The 1996 Survivor Series was made up of seven separate matches and Dwayne and his team were up fourth.

Dwayne made his dramatic entrance as Rocky Maivia in a shiny new outfit. It was blue and gold, with a neck sash and ribbons that reflected his Samoan and Hawaiian links. But despite the fancy threads, when his name was announced **hardly anyone clapped**.

Things didn't start brilliantly. Dwayne was thrown by the crowds, the lights, the music and sheer scale of the huge arena. The second he got into the ring he lost his bearings. He was **facing the wrong camera**, pointing and smiling with his back to the TV audience!

But then the match began, and Dwayne started to relax, concentrate on his moves and put his dodgy start behind him.

One by one, his team members were eliminated, leaving Rocky on his own to see off two remaining opponents. Now he needed to defeat two heels – Crush and Goldust. As the new kid, no one was expecting him to win, but **suddenly the crowd was behind him**, calling his name. Within minutes, the entire arena was shaking with shouts of 'Rocky, Rocky!'

'*Wow!*' one of the commentators said. '*This kid is a newcomer and he's already got 20,000 people chanting his name!*'

By then Crush and Goldust were taking turns to have a go at Rocky. He fought back, celebrating a series of successful punches with some crazy dance moves (WWE call it 'babyface fire'). But the fight wasn't over. Still with two against one, Goldust delivered a 'low blow' (a direct shot to the groin!) that brought Rocky to his knees. Crush yanked Rocky to his feet and Goldust pinned his arms round his back. Crush went in with a hard punch but Rocky got out of the way at the very last minute, and Crush hit Goldust instead!

Rocky didn't waste a second, he launched himself at Crush and pinned him to the mat. Now Rocky and Goldust (who had scrambled back to his feet while

Rocky was pinning Crush) were the only ones left standing, but Goldust was still so bewildered from Crush's punch that Rocky was able to lift him over his shoulder and slam him down with a nifty move called the shoulder breaker bang! And with that, Rocky had done it! He was **officially declared the winner**!

As the crowd leaped to their feet, Dwayne was on cloud nine. Unfortunately, he still hadn't figured out where the camera was, so all the viewers at home got to see of his celebration was the back of his head!

Back in Tampa, the Johnsons were jumping up and down hugging each other and wiping away tears of pride. It was an unforgettable night. And this was just the start.

He did it!

Bye-Bye, Babyface

After the Madison Square Garden win, the **offers of fights came pouring in**, and that winter, Dwayne took off on an international tour, visiting Europe and the Middle East. Dwayne hadn't travelled to any of these places before, but if he'd thought he'd be getting time out to see the sights, he was very much mistaken. The tour was **non-stop and gruelling**. Dwayne got homesick (he was missing Dany like crazy) and felt shy around his more experienced team-mates, so it was a good job Owen and Bret Hart were there to take him under their wing.

It did feel great to be earning a wage doing something he loved, and luckily the WWE had changed a great deal since his dad had wrestled for them. If you played your cards right and became popular with audiences, you could potentially earn a lot of money, **maybe even millions**. However, as one of WWE's newest faces, Dwayne was still some way off commanding a superstar salary.

Back in the US, the WWE bosses were keen for Rocky Maivia to try for the second most important title in the business (after the WWE Federation Championship): the Intercontinental Championship. Winning that would ensure every wrestling fan knew his name.

Dwayne was excited by the idea, but worried about how fans would react. He was still very new. Plus, babyfaces like him seemed to be going out of fashion. The most popular wrestler of the time was 'Stone Cold'

Steve Austin. Arrogant, rude and full of attitude, he was the ultimate heel, and audiences lapped up his bad behaviour. Were they really going to get behind an all-round good guy like Rocky? Dwayne wasn't so sure.

The match went ahead on 13th February 1997, and Rocky defeated a wrestler called Triple H as planned. At the time, that made him the **youngest wrestler ever** to take the Intercontinental Championship.

It was a fantastic moment, but just over a month later, he had to defend the title against a wrestler called The Sultan. It was one of the strangest matches of his entire career. Dwayne had the feeling that audiences were beginning to go off him, and there was a weird atmosphere in the air from the moment he entered the ring.

The Sultan was a Samoan wrestler and a notorious heel, who wore a mask and never spoke a word! When babyface Rocky made his entrance, smiling and waving, he was shocked to discover almost the entire arena had taken against him, chanting 'Rocky sucks! Rocky sucks!'

This didn't feel right. He was the good guy after all! The fans were supposed to be on his side. Why were they so against him?

Rocky beat The Sultan but it was hard to feel like a champion when **most people in the arena were booing him**.

Over the coming weeks, the booing and chanting continued. It was clear, to Dwayne at least, that the crowd had had enough of clean-cut, wholesome Rocky Maivia. Dwayne couldn't really blame them. He thought Rocky was bland and boring too!

Even so, **he began to panic**. If the audiences took against him altogether, his career could be over before it had even begun. So, when Dwayne injured his knee and was forced to take eight weeks off, he used his time wisely, to think about where his career was going, what he loved about wrestling, and what was wrong with 'Rocky Maivia'. That's when he came to a decision:

It was time for a makeover.

ACCEPTANCE AT LAST

Dwayne also used the break to do something he'd been wanting to do for a while – get married to Dany!

The pair had been dating for six years now and Dany's parents still refused to even meet Dwayne! As the wedding day got closer, Dwayne and Dany decided enough was enough and they went over to Dany's parents' apartment (they only lived a few minutes away) **intending to confront them**. Dwayne was ready for a fight, but much to his surprise, Dany's parents finally seemed to accept the relationship. In fact, in the run-up to the wedding, Dany's mum even got involved with the planning!

On 3rd May 1997, Dwayne and Dany were married. It was a beautiful day full of singing and dancing, that combined Dwayne's Samoan heritage with Dany's Cuban roots.

My mom even did an amazing wedding dance.

Along with the usual wedding cake, Dwayne had made a special request: **chocolate chip cookies**. Dozens of them were served up after dinner along with gallons of milk.

Many family members attended as well as friends with WWE connections, but quite a few others came along uninvited! According to Samoan tradition it's a mark of respect to turn up to the wedding of another countryman. The fact that so many Samoan dignitaries came to give their good wishes meant that Dwayne was really making an impression.

6   BAD-GUY DWAYNE

On Dwayne's first day back at work he was called into the WWE offices for a meeting with one of the bosses, Jim Ross.

'Dwayne,' he said. 'How do you feel about turning heel?'

It was like Jim had read Dwayne's mind. Dwayne had spent the past two months feeling unhappy about Rocky Maivia's squeaky-clean image and hoping his bosses would let him change tack. Now here they were, offering him **exactly what he wanted** on a plate.

'And if you're up for the challenge,' Jim added, 'we'd love you to join the Nation.'

The Nation (short for the Nation of Domination) was a faction of the WWE led by a wrestler known as Faarooq. It had a reputation for being hardcore and quite badly behaved! In other words, it was about as far away from clean-cut Rocky Maivia as you could get.

I liked the sound of that a lot!

By the end of the meeting, it was decided – Rocky Maivia was **officially a heel**. The next step was to let the audiences know.

Dwayne had a match that very night in Mississippi, and he was keen to try out his new persona without delay. He spent the afternoon plotting and planning, knowing that getting this right could change the entire course of his wrestling career.

A Heel Is Born

That night, Dwayne was due to interrupt a scheduled match between good guy Chainz and Faarooq (the head of the Nation of Domination), by performing a 'run-in' – climbing into the ring unexpectedly.

The crowd hadn't seen Rocky Maivia in over two months, and as he stepped out from behind the curtain, they just saw him as a babyface, here to help out fellow babyface, Chainz. However, Rocky Maivia wasn't smiling and waving as they were expecting. Instead he stomped into the ring with a snarl on his face, shaking his fist menacingly at the crowd. The audience were confused. **What was going on**?

The answer came when, instead of helping Chainz like everyone was expecting him to, Rocky slammed him on the mat and then celebrated by performing the Nation's official salute alongside Faarooq.

There was stunned silence for a while as the truth gradually dawned on the audience: Rocky Maivia had joined the Nation of Domination!

That's when **the booing began**, and this time Dwayne didn't mind. In fact, he lapped it up.

Dwayne's switch from babyface to heel really had come out of nowhere, so he asked his bosses if he could shoot a promo to explain himself.

Promos are a big part of the WWE. Before their matches, wrestlers often record short segments in character direct to camera. It's a great way for them to let the audience know who they are and what they're about.

Dwayne's promo would only last a few minutes, but **he spent hours** drafting and redrafting his speech. This was a huge opportunity to win over the audience and he had to get it exactly right.

On that week's WWE show, *Monday Night Raw*, Dwayne and his fellow Nation of Domination members entered the arena to chants of 'Rocky sucks!' It didn't put him off. Instead Dwayne fed off the crowd's energy, repeating their insults right back at them before launching into his speech.

Over the course of the next few minutes, Dwayne gave the fans a serious telling-off for the way they had treated him. They should be grateful to him he told them, for all the 'blood, sweat and tears' he'd put into his performances.

Microphone in hand, **Dwayne discovered he was in his element**. Confident, moody and not afraid to express his emotions, the new Rocky Maivia made complete sense to Dwayne. He finished by telling the fans he would earn their respect by any means possible, to a loud chorus of boos.

With that, the wholesome and clean-cut 'Rocky Maivia' was no more, and 'The Rock' was born. And the more The Rock railed against the WWE universe, from its fans to its most popular wrestlers, the more the audience responded.

WHAT MAKES THE ROCK?

Dwayne ditched his glitzy Rocky Maivia gear for simple black trunks and boots. The Rock didn't need to rely on a fancy costume to get attention. His athletic skill and personality would do the talking now.

Signature moves

The Rock Bottom:

The People's Elbow: This became one of the most famous and recognizable manoeuvres in WWE history.

Over the years, The Rock added a few extra flourishes:

elbow pad

Dwayne spent a lot of time planning material for promos and making notes of ideas for trash-talk insults, keeping things fresh and exciting for the audience.

Many of his quips became instantly quotable, with crowds of thousands often echoing them back to him. These are just a few of his most famous lines:

You want to go one-on-one with The Great One!

Can you smell what The Rock is cooking?

Just bring it!

Shine it up real nice, flip it sideways . . .

Why don't you drink a big, tall glass of shut-up juice?

Dwayne even trash-talked his opponents through song, staging 'Rock Concerts' where he played the guitar and mocked them with his witty lyrics. Audiences loved that. The Rock's fellow wrestlers weren't quite so keen – he was usually making brutal jokes at their expense.

I will be bold and beat Stone Cold, And do it Rock's way.

It only took a few months for The Rock to become **one of the most popular heels** in the WWE. The fans loved to hate him, and The Rock loved to be 'hated'. He delighted the crowds with his outrageous speeches and knack for picking fights with pretty much everyone in the WWE. Now when he was in the ring, he could strut about confidently and be as arrogant, cocky and argumentative as he liked, and enjoy every second of it.

Monday-Night Wars

In the 1990s, the WWE were not the only ones producing wrestling TV shows. A rival promotion called World Championship Wrestling began screening a weekly TV show called *Monday Nitro*, designed to go directly head to head with WWE's *Monday Night Raw*. Soon *Nitro* was beating *Raw* in the ratings and WWE were desperate to win back their viewers.

Their solution was to make their show as violent, gritty and outrageous as possible. It was a gamble. The WWE had a long history of providing family-friendly entertainment, but the bosses felt it was **a risk worth taking** and surged ahead with the new-look show.

With his endless supply of witty put-downs and razor-sharp one-liners, The Rock was the perfect fit for the new-style *Monday Night Raw* and soon he was appearing every week, taking every opportunity to be as **rude, arrogant and downright shocking** as possible.

The audiences came flocking back and the five years that followed became known as the 'Attitude Era' – one of wrestling's golden ages that produced dozens of stars who entertained fans every week with their crazy antics. These included:

FAMOUS FEUDS

The Attitude Era was notable for featuring some of the fiercest rivalries in WWE history, and over the course of his wrestling career, The Rock clashed with the some of the biggest names in the business. Sometimes he won, sometimes he lost, but he could always be relied upon to **make magic** the second the microphone was in his hand, a talent that came in particularly handy when he found himself up against the legendary 'Stone Cold' Steve Austin.

In 1997 'Stone Cold' Steve was one of the biggest names in wrestling. He'd recently taken the Intercontinental title off Owen Hart and was riding high. One time, he was in the ring cutting a new promo when in walked The Rock. He had a microphone in his hand and challenged the furious Steve for the championship, live on air.

He finished by saying:

If you do accept my challenge, then your bottom line will say: Stone Cold has-been. Compliments of . . . The Rock!

Steve accepted The Rock's challenge and the **greatest rivalry** in wrestling history was born. Even Dwayne didn't know how to explain it, but something incredible happened when the two were in the ring together. It helped that (in front of the cameras at least) The Rock and 'Stone Cold' Steve hated each other! Behind the scenes they actually got on pretty well, but the audiences loved their rivalry so much, they could never risk fans knowing they were friends.

The highlight of their feud was the infamous 'pager incident'. It took place in November 1997 during an episode of *Monday Night Raw*. The Rock was in the ring when his pager went off with a mocking message from Steve. Seconds later Steve appeared unexpectedly out of nowhere and jumped on The Rock, making the crowd go wild.

Steve won that match – it had all been planned, of course – but Dwayne didn't care, because the video clip of the scene quickly became one of the **most famous** in sport entertainment history.

Dwayne was on the top of the world, but he wasn't going to let himself get comfortable. No matter how much success he enjoyed, he was always on the lookout for the next opportunity.

GO, ROCK

STONE COLD!

DWAYNE SPENDS SOME DOUGH

Remember the lists of goals Dwayne wrote down back when he was wrestling in Memphis? Well, by 2000 every single one of them had come true, and, yes, **he had become a millionaire**. He wasn't just getting a hefty salary from the WWE (rumoured to be around 13 million dollars), he also got a percentage of all the merchandise sales.

In direct response to The Rock's soaring fame and popularity, the WWE had brought out a range of products bearing his image – everything from T-shirts and posters to action figures and video games. It proved a merchandising gold mine. By the early 2000s the WWE was taking over **120 million dollars per year** in merchandise sales alone, thanks almost entirely to The Rock's reputation.

He'd even found the time to write an autobiography. *The Rock Says . . .* was published in October 1999 and rocketed straight to the top of the *New York Times* bestseller list where it stayed for a stunning 20 weeks. Not bad for a guy who was once almost thrown out of college!

After all those years of scraping and struggling, Dwayne loved being rich and not having to worry about money any more. Having made his first million, Dwayne told his dad to quit his truck-driving job. He lavished both his parents with gifts and treated himself to a few nice things too. As a teenager, Dwayne had got it into his head that successful people owned Rolex watches, so the moment he started earning big money, he splashed out on the **flashiest Rolex** he could get his hands on. He broke it almost straight away, but he's loved Rolex watches ever since and now has a huge collection.

Dwayne also loves buying cars and trucks, not just for himself, but for his family too. Over the years, he's given new sets of wheels to everyone from his dad to his cousins.

His new-found wealth also meant he could finally give Dany the sort of life he'd always promised her. They moved from their cramped apartment in Miami to a big house in a fancy neighbourhood. Then, in 2001, they **welcomed a daughter**, Simone, into the world.

Knowing I could always provide for Dany and Simone felt great.

Of course, there were some downsides to fame. Dwayne couldn't nip to the mall for a burger without being mobbed by fans and he was recognized pretty much everywhere he went. He was also working incredibly hard. He spent 225 days of the year on the road. On top of the matches themselves, there were countless TV and radio interviews and personal appearances. Despite his quick temper, The Rock was **a great interviewee**, full of natural charm, wit and charisma. He was always in demand.

Dwayne was grateful for the interviews and he knew all too well that his success was down to the support of his fans. He never refused an autograph, even if he was tired or grumpy and just wanted to be left alone to eat his dinner in peace. Anytime he felt resentful, he thought back to his time in Calgary, sleeping on a dirty mattress and surviving on nothing but spaghetti, and remembered just how lucky he was.

7 DWAYNE HEADS TO HOLLYWOOD

Dwayne had always liked the idea of acting. As a kid, he'd watched the film *Indiana Jones* and fantasized about becoming a Hollywood star, like Harrison Ford.

As a teenager he'd even auditioned for a small role in a soap opera. He didn't get it. After that, seeing as he'd never taken any acting classes and didn't know anyone in the film business, he'd assumed acting was out of the question for him.

However, that was all about to change. With his new-found fame, the lack of coaching and contacts didn't seem to matter any more. Plus, acting was a big part of the WWE anyway, so it wasn't like Dwayne didn't have any experience. The more he thought about it, the more a move from wrestling to acting seemed to make a whole lot of sense. They were both about connecting with an audience, and Dwayne knew he **had a special knack** for that.

The transition wasn't going to be simple. In fact, being recognizable as The Rock could actually work against him. Wrestling legends like Andre the Giant and Hulk Hogan had appeared in movies, but they'd never really been able to shake off their wrestling pasts. Dwayne knew he'd have to **work twice as hard** as most actors to convince audiences if he was playing a new character. Then again, he was used to hard work. So, when an opportunity came knocking in 1999, he grabbed it, eager to prove himself – again.

THE ROCK PLAYS ROCKY

That '70s Show was a popular TV comedy about a group of teenagers growing up in the 1970s. The role wasn't exactly a stretch for Dwayne. He'd be playing a wrestler. One he actually knew quite well: Rocky Johnson – **his own dad**! Dwayne jumped at the chance and donned an Afro wig, stick-on moustache and sideburns to capture his dad's seventies style. He had an absolute blast on set.

Despite the fun, Dwayne assumed it was a one-off. So he really wasn't expecting a call from the producers of *Saturday Night Live* (*SNL*), America's infamous late-night comedy sketch show. They'd seen Dwayne's performance on *That '70s Show*, they'd seen his over-the-top promos, and they thought he might just have something special.

The call was a BIG deal. *SNL* goes out live every Saturday night, regularly attracting **over nine million viewers**. Not only that, the producers didn't just want Dwayne to make a quick appearance – they wanted him to host the entire show!

Over the years, *SNL* has attracted plenty of big-name celebrities as hosts (more recently, Kristen Stewart, Harry Styles and RuPaul have taken on the role). Dwayne didn't need asking twice! This was a massive opportunity to reach a whole new audience, and he agreed to take part immediately.

With just one condition.

No wrestling.

Dwayne was hugely proud of his career with the WWE, but he knew this was a golden opportunity for viewers to see him in a different light.

The producers agreed, and a date was confirmed for the recording. Dwayne was excited and nervous at the same time. As the name suggests, *SNL* goes out live. There'd be no retakes if anything went wrong. He'd only get one chance to make an impression, and if he messed up, there'd be no opportunity to put it right.

The episode began with a monologue straight to camera. Thanks to all the promos he'd recorded over the previous couple of years, Dwayne breezed through it and got some **big laughs** along the way. Next came the sketches.

Bouncing from one crazy skit to another, Dwayne 'The Rock' Johnson:

⭐ Played an undercover police officer disguised as a woman.

⭐ Played Clark Kent!

⭐ Crooned Elvis Presley's 'Are You Lonesome Tonight?' with the help of a couple of friends.

Who knew The Rock could sing so sweetly?

The audience loved it, and **Dwayne had an absolute ball**. He didn't just thrill the studio audience; fans of *SNL* watching at home suddenly saw him in a totally new light too. The show had worked out exactly as he'd hoped. It was clear to everyone that Dwayne Johnson was much more than just The Rock. Dwayne couldn't wait to show them exactly how much more.

He'd been performing as The Rock for three years now, and although he loved his alter ego, getting to play lots of different characters sounded like an exciting challenge. Luckily, Hollywood agreed, and it wasn't long before the movie scouts came calling.

First, he was offered the lead in a sci-fi action film, then a comic-book-hero script, but Dwayne didn't just jump at the first opportunity. He'd learned lessons from his wrestling days, and he knew if he was going to go into acting properly, he needed to pick the right part.

Finally, a role came up that made perfect sense to Dwayne – the Scorpion King in *The Mummy Returns* [12].

Dwayne was keen to accept the role for two big reasons. Number one, the first *Mummy* film had been a big hit so it was likely that this one would be too. Number two, unlike the other offers he'd had, he wouldn't be taking on the leading role, and **that was fine by Dwayne**. He felt ready to give film acting a go, not to carry a whole film on his shoulders. Dwayne was prepared to throw himself into the role; he just needed to clarify something first.

> *I didn't want to do the eyebrow thing. I didn't think it was fitting. Not for this movie.*

SHIVERING IN THE SAHARA

Dwayne's Hollywood debut didn't start well. *The Mummy Returns* was shooting in the Sahara Desert and Dwayne arrived on set with a bad case of food poisoning and heatstroke. **He felt dreadful**. While the rest of cast and crew were wearing shorts in the 46-degree heat, Dwayne was shivering beneath a pile of blankets. The last thing he wanted was to shoot an action scene with no top on, but luckily, thanks to his time in the wrestling ring, he had plenty of experience of blocking out pain and getting on with the job in hand, no matter how rotten he was feeling. When it was time to shoot his scene, he threw the blankets off, gritted his teeth and got stuck in. Then he'd run back to his cave of blankets the moment the director yelled 'cut'.

As it happened, the producers were actually really impressed by Dwayne's dedication against the odds, and they thought he performed with charisma too. Before the filming had even finished, they got in touch with Dwayne's agent to offer him more work. A lot more work: they wanted to take his Scorpion King character and give him **his very own movie**!

Dwayne appeared in *The Mummy Returns* for just 15 minutes, and only spoke a single line of dialogue (and that was in ancient Egyptian, no less – '*Haku machente!*') but from the reactions of the critics and the audiences, it was clear he absolutely **stole the show**.

Boosted by the success of *The Mummy Returns* and flattered by the faith the studio had in him to carry an entire movie, Dwayne signed the contract for *The Scorpion King*[15] and instantly became the highest-paid actor in a first-time leading role in Hollywood history. The studio was paying him a whopping $5.5 million!

Dwayne Takes The Lead

Taking on an entire film was scary, but at least Dwayne already knew his character and, as ever, he was prepared to put in 110 per cent to prove he was worth the hefty price tag. He'd always played a role in the wrestling ring, and he was used to portraying big emotions like anger, fear, shock, surprise and pain, but anything smaller or more subtle was really going to test his skills. How could he react convincingly when the Scorpion King's brother was killed right in front of him, for example? It was a whole new challenge for Dwayne, so an acting coach called Larry Moss was brought on board to help him. With Larry's encouragement and guidance, he was able to not only tone things down, but also to tap into emotions that he'd never been in tune with in the wrestling ring.

'*Sadness is something I'd never really portrayed,*' Dwayne explained once. '*So, I found that sadness. And, to be honest with you, 15 minutes later – bawling, bawling like a baby . . .*'

With Larry's help, by the time Dwayne had to shoot his brother's death scene, he had **no problem tearing up** on demand.

But he didn't quite leave his wrestling persona behind him. Once Dwayne relaxed on set, he became a bit of a joker. In the build-up to a love scene with co-star Kelly Hu, both actors were nervous, but Dwayne found a way to lighten the mood.

Dwayne had brought in a **fart machine** and got one of the crew to operate it. It made the entire cast and crew crack up and the take was completely ruined, but suddenly everyone relaxed. After that, shooting the scene was a breeze.

The Scorpion King was released in 2002 and became a solid box-office hit. Dwayne earned praise for his performance, and an unexpected honour: Madame Tussaud's wax museum in New York City created a statue of him!

Everything was going brilliantly, and offers of more parts were flooding in. Dwayne was delighted, but he was careful choosing his next project.

He'd taken time out from the WWE to shoot *The Scorpion King*, and although he loved the experience of being on set, he wasn't quite ready to say goodbye to wrestling. When he returned to the ring, however, it seemed **things had changed**, and Dwayne was shocked to discover that his fans' loyalty had been tested. They suspected their hero was on track for big things in

Hollywood and had a feeling wrestling was going to have to take a backseat, at least for a while.

Their suspicions were right. If Dwayne was going to be taken seriously as a film actor, he knew he was going to need to give it everything. It was a big, scary decision, but when his contract with WWE came to an end, Dwayne **didn't ask for it to be renewed**. It was time to stop playing it safe and start taking some risks.

8   DWAYNE TAKES CONTROL

Over the next few years, Dwayne 'The Rock' Johnson appeared in various films playing:

⭐ A bounty hunter in an action comedy called *The Rundown* [15]. It was set in Brazil, but filmed in Hawaii, so Dwayne felt right at home.

⭐ An ex-army sergeant battling crime in his hometown in *Walking Tall* [15].

⭐ A marine on a mission to Mars in the sci-fi movie, *Doom* [15].

⭐ A football star discovering he has a daughter in family comedy *The Game Plan* [U].

The movies did well enough at the box office, but they didn't get great reviews. Dwayne was disappointed. He'd started out with a big budget for *The Scorpion King* and now each new movie he made had a smaller budget and less enthusiastic write-up. His acting career seemed to be **heading down the toilet**. Something had to change.

His agent had some suggestions:

Dwayne did as he was told, and it was a slimmed-down version of plain old Dwayne Johnson who appeared in the

Lose weight, ditch the wrestling image and drop 'The Rock'.

action comedy *Get Smart* 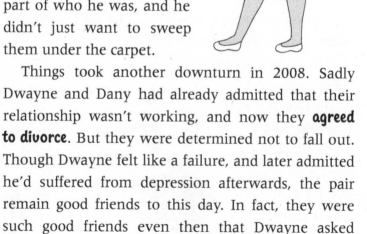⑫ in 2008. Then, in *Tooth Fairy* ㉊, Dwayne was an ice hockey player (he had to learn how to skate!) who's accused of ruining children's dreams and sentenced to serve time as a tooth fairy – complete with fairy wings and, at one point, a pink tutu!

Something just doesn't feel right . . .

Dwayne worked as hard as ever on these roles, but he was a big guy and trying to fight against nature seemed disrespectful to both his wrestling background and his Samoan roots. They were both such a big part of who he was, and he didn't just want to sweep them under the carpet.

Things took another downturn in 2008. Sadly Dwayne and Dany had already admitted that their relationship wasn't working, and now they **agreed to divorce**. But they were determined not to fall out. Though Dwayne felt like a failure, and later admitted he'd suffered from depression afterwards, the pair remain good friends to this day. In fact, they were such good friends even then that Dwayne asked

Dany to become **his manager**. She'd been involved in his career right from the start, she was highly experienced in the world of finance and, whatever had happened in their marriage, he knew she'd always have his best interests at heart.

SMART DECISIONS

In 2011, with Dany at the helm, Dwayne got a new agent – one of Hollywood's most powerful: Ari Emanuel. Straight away, Ari seemed to get where Dwayne was coming from, and Dwayne was relieved someone was finally listening to him.

If I want to be called The Rock, I'll be called The Rock. If I want to go back to wrestling, I'll go back to wrestling. It's all the same guy. Ari got that.

Indeed, Ari gave his blessing when, just a few months later, Dwayne did decide to go back to wrestling for a bit. He carried on acting too, only this time, with Ari's support, he was finally doing things on his terms.

Dwayne knew that if he was going to have a long-lasting career, his next film needed to be a huge hit. So, when he accepted a role in the fifth instalment of the Fast and the Furious series – *Fast Five* [12] – a lot of people were puzzled. Why would he share star billing with Vin Diesel and Paul Walker? There'd already been four Fast and Furious films. What was exciting about yet another sequel?

Dwayne just **had a hunch** this was the right move for him. Sharing the star billing meant he didn't have the pressure of carrying the entire film alone, and he was excited about breathing new life into the series.

Playing a Diplomatic Security Service agent was also right up Dwayne's street. It was another action-heavy role with fight scenes and car chases galore. But the script also offered lots of opportunities for Dwayne to showcase his knack for comedy, especially when he played face to face with fellow action star Vin Diesel.

The film was a huge hit, earning great reviews and making an almighty $626 million at the box office. Most excitingly of all, almost everyone agreed its success was largely thanks to Dwayne:

EMPIRE

How to reignite an ageing franchise? Drop The Rock on it.

The best thing, by far, in Fast Five... Dwayne Johnson hulks through the movie leaving testosterone trails in his wake.

2013: A Very Good Year

Now his movie career was really going places, Dwayne had **no intention of slowing down**! In 2013 he appeared in no fewer than FIVE films, working back-to-back pretty much the entire year. OK, the true crime drama *Empire State* ⑮ didn't do so well, but his other four movies were hits:

⭐ In *Snitch* ⑫ there were fight scenes and a dramatic car chase, but Dwayne impressed the critics with his 'more thoughtful' performance.

⭐ In *G.I. Joe: Retaliation* ⑫ he played a heavy machine gunner called Roadblock. The film was packed with action: the big cliff battle scene was so complex it took two whole months to film!

⭐ In *Pain & Gain* ⑮ Dwayne played a recently released convict. He hit the gym and bulked up for the role. He got so big, in one scene, when he had to ride in another character's car, the T-bar had to be removed to make room for him!

But I still look cool, right?

Size Matters

Dwayne was already a BIG guy before bulking up! Want to know how big he got? Here are the (massive) stats:

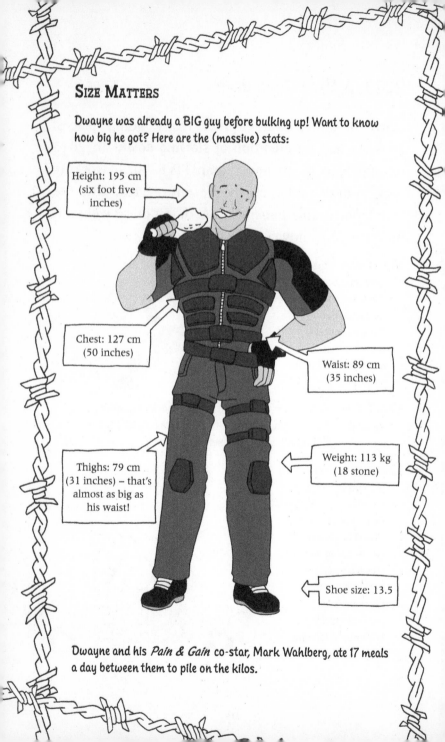

Height: 195 cm (six foot five inches)

Chest: 127 cm (50 inches)

Waist: 89 cm (35 inches)

Thighs: 79 cm (31 inches) – that's almost as big as his waist!

Weight: 113 kg (18 stone)

Shoe size: 13.5

Dwayne and his *Pain & Gain* co-star, Mark Wahlberg, ate 17 meals a day between them to pile on the kilos.

Closing 2013 in style, Dwayne was back in his role as Luke Hobbs in the sixth Fast and Furious film, predictably named *Fast and Furious 6*. The film's massive $260-million budget was mostly spent on some impressive stunt sequences. One estimate says that **350 cars** were crashed, wrecked or otherwise destroyed over the course of the shoot. No one worried too much about all those wasted vehicles once the movie grossed over $787 million at the box office!

In 2013, film-goers spent a total of **$1.3 billion** to watch Dwayne in action – more than any other actor in the world!

9 DWAYNE – ACTION MAN

Thanks to his athletic background, Dwayne is a natural action hero. He likes to do as much of the movie stunt work himself as possible, but **there are limits**! When the stunts get too dangerous, Dwayne calls in the expert: his stunt double, Tanoai Reed. Tanoai specializes in chariot driving, car work, air ramps, flying wire, swords, fights, mixed martial arts and scuba. He's been working with Dwayne ever since *The Scorpion King*.

Obviously, a stunt double has to look like the actor they're working for, so it certainly helps that Tanoai and Dwayne share the same Samoan heritage. They even worked out **they're related**! Their great-grandfathers were cousins!

To keep a similar shape, Dwayne and Tanoai share a similar fitness routine. It's not for the faint-hearted!

THE FITNESS EXPLAINED

I don't look the way I do by pure luck. It's hard work keeping these muscles.

First, I set my alarm for 4 a.m., and go for a run. While I'm running, I get my head in gear for the day ahead.

If I can't run outside, I'll train on a treadmill with my headphones on.

Listening to Kanye West, NWA, Kid Rock

Here comes the good bit – breakfast! It's huge, and it involves steak, eggs and porridge.

Next it's workout time. No, running definitely wasn't enough. I head to my private gym – I call it the 'Iron Paradise'. If I'm away on a shoot, I insist on having access to a gym (and if the facilities don't look good enough, I'll just bring my own 'Iron Paradise').

Equipment weighs over 18,000 kg

When I lift weights, I concentrate on different muscle groups – different roles require different body shapes:

Pain for gain.

⭐ For demigod Hercules I had to bulk up.

⭐ For the fire fighter in *San Andreas* ⑫, I focused on my core.

Fuelling this body takes an awful lot of calories, so I have to find the time to eat up to seven meals a day! A typical day's menu could include:

DWAYNE'S DAILY MENU

two steaks	plus loads of vegetables
two chicken breasts	potatoes
a kilo of cod	rice
13 egg whites	salad
	several protein shakes.

This totals around $4\frac{1}{2}$ kilos of food a day (you probably eat more like 1 to $1\frac{1}{2}$ kilos).
Junk food is a no-no . . .

Except on a cheat day when I let myself eat pancakes, pizza and maybe a platter of brownies!

Seven Bucks

With so many successful movies under his belt, Dwayne was now **a very rich man** indeed. He could afford to do something productive with his money, and he wanted to have as much control over his career and the sort of projects he was involved in as possible. That's why, in 2012, Dwayne and Dany had decided to set up a production company together. As if life wasn't busy enough! The company aimed to bring exciting yet relatable stories to film and TV. Dwayne might have had trouble coming up with his first wrestling name, but he had no problem naming their company. He called it: Seven Bucks Productions.

Remember that awful time, back on page 53, when he'd been cut from the Calgary Stampeders? That was 17 years earlier, but Dwayne could remember how he'd felt at the time **like it was yesterday**, and the desperation of having only seven dollars to his name.

In fact, he used that very story to introduce each episode of a reality TV series he and Dany produced called *Wake-up Call*.

By the time I was 23 years old, I had multiple arrests . . . My dream of being a pro football player was shattered. I had seven bucks in my pocket . . . I started over. This show is about real people picking themselves up and saying, 'I can do better'.

With a nod to Dwayne's own past struggles, the show helped people to realize their dreams.

Although the show only ran for one season, Dwayne was **enormously proud** of it and, by 2015, he felt ready to start producing comedy-drama, and was soon scouting around for interesting projects. The second he read the script for *Ballers*, he knew he wanted to be involved, not just as a producer but in front of the camera too. The role of Spencer Strasmore, a retired NFL player who has to navigate his new career as the financial manager of other NFL players, was perfect for Dwayne. Later the writers said he'd been their *only* choice for the part.

Playing Spencer gave Dwayne the chance to explore what might have happened if his football career had actually taken off. The opening credits even featured actual footage of the young Dwayne kicking a ball around.

It was an opportunity to not only embrace culture, not only embrace ambition, not only embrace success – which we do in the show – but also embrace the failures, which is a key and critical thing in life, to learn from them.

The show was a **massive success**, running for five seasons on HBO and attracting cameo appearances from some of the biggest names in the NFL (athletes like Terrell Suggs, Victor Cruz and DeSean Jackson). Plus, everyone agreed that Dwayne brought 'depth and charm' to his role.

ANIMATED DWAYNE

Who'd have thought a big guy like Dwayne would be a **huge fan** of animated films? *Aladdin* and *The Little Mermaid* are two of his absolute favourites, and he'd always wanted to appear in a full-length Disney feature. So, when the bosses at Disney asked if he'd like to be the voice behind the animated character of Maui in the 2016 film *Moana* ᴾᴳ, he couldn't believe his luck. It was a gamble, though, because the film was also a musical, and Dwayne had never done one of those before either.

Recording a voice role is very different from a live action movie. Actors can't use their own facial expressions or body language to bring a character to life and often have to record their lines individually so can't bounce off other characters. Dwayne was **so nervous**, he kept asking his fellow actors if he was doing OK.

Voice acting has to be the hardest kind of acting there is.

There were a few things about the film that made it easier for Dwayne, however. Firstly, *Moana* is set in the Polynesian Pacific and, secondly, Maui is **absolutely huge** (he is a demigod after all) with plenty of tattoos! So, Dwayne was at home with the environment, and he certainly looked the part, even if no one would see him.

With his hulking build, intricate tattoos and long flowing hair, Maui looked **strangely like Dwayne's grandfather**, Peter Maivia, and Dwayne happily pictured Peter as he recorded his lines. The directors were keen for Dwayne to put his stamp on the role, so they incorporated his signature moves into the animation. Maui raises an eyebrow when he first meets Moana – a direct reference to The People's Eyebrow that Dwayne had tried to shake off a few years earlier (he didn't mind it this time round). And, of course, Dwayne has no shortage of tattoos.

THE TATTOOS EXPLAINED

It's a rite of passage for young men in the Polynesian, Maori and Samoan cultures of the South Pacific (see page 14) to get a traditional tribal tattoo telling the story of their forefathers.

The word 'tattoo' even comes from the Samoan word *tatau*. The male Samoan tattoo (known as a *pe'a*) runs front and back from the waist to the knees.

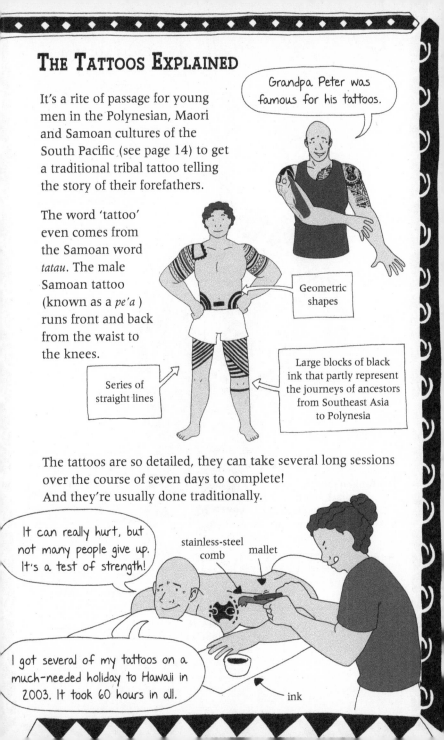

Grandpa Peter was famous for his tattoos.

Geometric shapes

Series of straight lines

Large blocks of black ink that partly represent the journeys of ancestors from Southeast Asia to Polynesia

The tattoos are so detailed, they can take several long sessions over the course of seven days to complete! And they're usually done traditionally.

It can really hurt, but not many people give up. It's a test of strength!

stainless-steel comb

mallet

I got several of my tattoos on a much-needed holiday to Hawaii in 2003. It took 60 hours in all.

ink

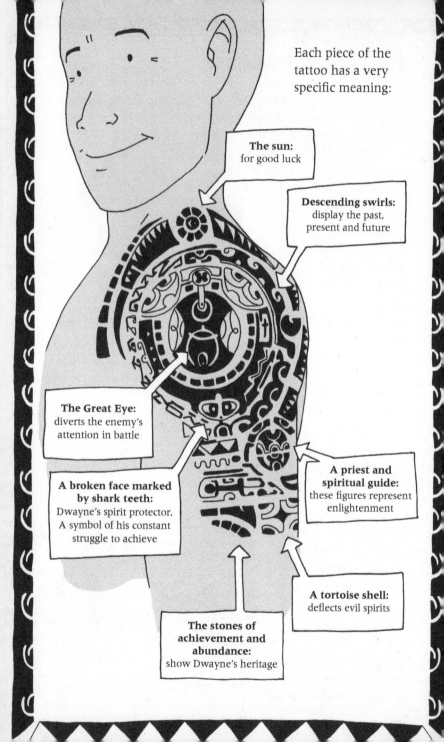

Each piece of the tattoo has a very specific meaning:

The sun:
for good luck

Descending swirls:
display the past, present and future

The Great Eye:
diverts the enemy's attention in battle

A broken face marked by shark teeth:
Dwayne's spirit protector. A symbol of his constant struggle to achieve

A priest and spiritual guide:
these figures represent enlightenment

A tortoise shell:
deflects evil spirits

The stones of achievement and abundance:
show Dwayne's heritage

Tattoos might be all about strength, but Dwayne also has a more light-hearted side, and it came out when, as Maui, he sang the incredibly catchy song 'You're Welcome'. A recording was released as a single, which **ended up going platinum**.

The song was a big hit with Dwayne's family too. After recovering from the disappointment of his divorce years earlier, Dwayne got together with singer-songwriter Lauren Hashian. In 2015, they welcomed their first daughter, Jasmine, then Tiana came along in 2018. Dwayne regularly uses 'You're Welcome' as a bedtime song for his girls, who haven't quite got to grips with the idea that their dad is a superstar. In a series of fun videos, with his youngest daughter on his lap, Dwayne sings along with the soundtrack, but little Tiana just can't believe her daddy is the voice of Maui!

Is Daddy Maui?

NO-O-O!

FUN IN THE JUNGLE

Meanwhile, Seven Bucks was having its ups and downs. Producing was still very new to Dwayne, but knowing some things might fail wasn't going to stop him from giving them a try.

Luckily, he didn't have to wait too long for a smash hit. Dwayne could spot a good story a mile away, and as soon as he read the script for a sequel to the 1995 film *Jumanji*, he just **knew he was on to a winner** and jumped at the chance to co-produce with Sony, one of the biggest entertainment companies in the world.

The plot focuses on a group of teenagers who come across the video game *Jumanji* 21 years after the events of the original 1995 film. They find themselves trapped in the game as a set of avatars who – if they ever want to escape and return home – need to work together to complete a special quest. Called *Jumanji: Welcome to the Jungle* (12A), the movie went into production in 2016.

Dwayne had **huge fun** playing an underconfident high-school student stuck in the body of hunky explorer Dr Xander Bravestone, and the film included lots of jokey references to Dwayne Johnson's wrestling and football career:

★ In a fight scene, Bravestone dispatches a henchman using one of The Rock's famous moves – the Rock Bottom.

★ Fridge – one of the other teenagers who's on the school football team – wears a football jersey that reads #94. This was Dwayne's jersey number when he played for the University of Miami.

★ Bravestone is 195 cm (6 feet 5 inches) tall and weighs over 122 kg (19 stone), sharing Dwayne's impressive stats (he gained a few extra pounds for the role).

★ At one point, Bravestone refers to himself in third person – just as The Rock used to do – and the other characters all comment on it.

Back in Hawaii to shoot the movie, Dwayne felt right at home, though some of the cast and crew had difficulty coping with the creepy-crawlies.

It was an intense three-month shoot, but when *Jumanji: Welcome to the Jungle* was released in 2017 it won over audiences and critics straight away, quickly becoming one of the **highest-grossing films** in Sony Pictures' history.

The movie paved the way for a string of projects for Seven Bucks. There was a sequel, *Jumanji: The Next Level* ⑫Ⓐ, in 2019, as well as *Rampage* ⑫Ⓐ, *Shazam!* ⑫Ⓐ and *Skyscraper* ⑫Ⓐ.

Dwayne took the lead in *Rampage* with an interesting set of co-stars. Based on a video game, he played a primatologist fighting to save his best friend, George, **an albino gorilla**, who's mutating into a monster.

Dwayne was already an animal lover, having brought two French bulldog puppies, Brutus and Hobbs, to the family home in 2015 (almost immediately he had to dive in and rescue one of them from the swimming pool). So, he was up for getting on with gorillas and went to meet some to prepare for the part. He even **learned some sign language** so he could communicate with them, and it's used in the movie.

Dwayne was producer on the movie too, and when he discovered that George's character was to be killed off at the end, he put his foot down. Dwayne likes a happy ending. He wants his audience to go away smiling. In the end the director saw things Dwayne's way, and George lived to rampage again.

In *Skyscraper*, Dwayne played a one-legged FBI agent trying to rescue his family from the world's tallest skyscraper and, technically, he was the lead. In fact, the real star of the show was the skyscraper itself. The Pearl was created almost entirely through computer-generated imagery (CGI) and at 1,066 metres (3,497 feet) high it was **taller than any existing building on the planet**.

The film included plenty of larger-than-life stunts too. The movie's poster shows Dwayne leaping from a crane and heading for the smashed-open window of a massive, burning skyscraper. Dwayne shared the poster via Twitter, and it was retweeted 1,700 times in five days. That wasn't unusual for a Dwayne Johnson tweet, but then people began discussing the believability of the image (there's no way he could really have made the jump). When someone posted a mock-up of the poster showing where Dwayne should *really* have landed it was retweeted **15,000 times** in five days.

It's all good publicity!

Where Dwayne landed in the movie

Where Dwayne should have landed

IT'S PERSONAL

A lot of the projects Seven Bucks takes on are personal for Dwayne, but *Fighting with My Family* ⑫ⓐ came right from the heart. Dwayne knew it was never going to be a blockbuster and, at first, no studios were interested, but he **loved the story** too much to let it go. The movie, a classic underdog tale, is about an English wrestler from Norwich called Paige (real name Saraya-Jade Bevis). Like Dwayne, Paige comes from a wrestling family and found fame with the WWE. She even won her very first match on the main WWE roster, just like Dwayne did back in 1996. Dwayne relished the opportunity to pull back the curtain and show viewers just how much hard work goes into professional wrestling. He produced the movie, but **couldn't resist** appearing as himself, popping up at various points throughout the film. It wasn't a huge hit, and Dwayne wasn't surprised by that, but he was proud that the critics praised *Fighting with My Family* for its 'wit' and 'big heart'.

In 2017, a documentary he produced, called *A Rock and a Hard Place*, was also very personal. It followed a group of young offenders who were given the opportunity to trade a long prison sentence for a fresh start by completing a Boot Camp called the Miami-Dade County Corrections & Rehabilitation Program. The documentary chronicled the boys over a harsh six months in which drill sergeants pushed them to their limit, at the same time encouraging them to learn from their past mistakes and become valuable members of society, who were less likely to reoffend and find themselves back in prison.

It was directly inspired by Dwayne's own experience with crime as a teenager. *'I always want to remind people of my past, because it is directly responsible for who I am today,'* Dwayne has said. *'It's undeniable that I'm a product of those tough times. I am a product of the most challenging times of my life. And that's the value of them.*

They shape you and they mould you, and so I was formed by these lessons at a very young age.' Indeed, Dwayne's peptalks with the young inmates were one of the most inspiring parts of the documentary.

It seemed Dwayne could turn his hand to just about anything, and his contribution to the movie business did not go unnoticed. At the end of 2017 he received a rather exciting telephone call.

Mr Johnson, we'd like you on our sidewalk.

Wow!

The Hollywood Walk of Fame, in Los Angeles, California, consists of over 2,600 brass stars that are embedded in the pavement. Each star honours a person who has made a substantial contribution to the entertainment industry. Getting a Hollywood star basically means you've really made it.

DWAYNE JOHNSON

Dwayne was thrilled when, on 13th December 2017, he was officially awarded the 2,624th star. Hundreds of fans turned up to watch the grand unveiling. And guess who his star is next to? None other than wrestling legend Vince McMahon (founder of the WWE) on one side and, er . . . Kermit the Frog on the other!

Of all Dwayne's projects, his most personal so far, has to be the sitcom, *Young Rock*. It's based on Dwayne's adventures as a child and teenager (many of which are featured here!), and it launched in early 2021, to rave reviews.

Mr Popular

You don't get to be that famous without coming into contact with a lot of people. And lots of those people have **great things to say** about Dwayne as a wrestler, actor, producer and businessman:

He's like this huge ball of charisma and muscle and teeth just flying at you.

He's literally a demigod in real life!

He's grinding every day ... There's an intensity when you're working around him and you can see it and feel it in the air.

He's always expanding, and he just gets better as he goes, like a flower that never stops blooming.

Jeffrey Dean Morgan
(Dwayne's co-star in *Rampage*)

Auli'i Cravalho
(the voice of *Moana*)

Alvin Streeter
(Dwayne's stand-in on *Jumanji*)

Zac Efron
(Dwayne's co-star in *Baywatch*)

You guys!

GETTING THE LOOK

A big part of Dwayne's life involves promoting his work. At the interviews, premieres, parties and business meetings he attends all over the world, he has to make sure he looks his best. Being big has lots of advantages, but some disadvantages too – Dwayne hasn't always found it easy to know what to wear.

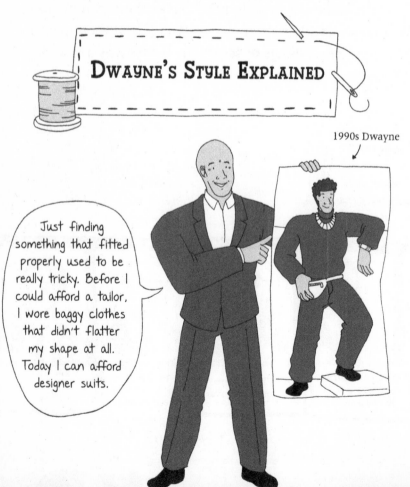

DWAYNE'S STYLE EXPLAINED

1990s Dwayne

Just finding something that fitted properly used to be really tricky. Before I could afford a tailor, I wore baggy clothes that didn't flatter my shape at all. Today I can afford designer suits.

But I like to dress casual too . . .

Sometimes I have a stylist, but in 2016, I launched a partnership with athletic brand Under Armour called 'Project Rock'. The first item we released (a duffel bag) sold out within hours!

Since then, we've partnered on everything from clothes and shoes to wireless headphones, all under the Project Rock banner.

In May 2018 a pair of Project Rock shoes sold out in just 30 minutes!

Some of the money earned from Project Rock goes to an organization called Team Rubicon that trains military veterans to help out in disaster zones and humanitarian crises. And that's not the only way Dwayne is helping out . . .

10 BUSINESSMAN DWAYNE

As you've probably worked out already, Dwayne is always busy. Generally it's with film work, but he hasn't completely ruled out a return to the ring. He doesn't have a contract with the WWE any more, but he regularly pops up at shows (often as a surprise). He likes to have his fingers in lots of pies.

With an incredible 277 million followers on Instagram, and 73 million more on Facebook and Twitter, it's safe to say

Dwayne has a lot of fans

and he's grateful to every single one of them!

I wouldn't be where I am today without them.

It's one of the reasons he's always looking for ways to give back. In 2006, Dwayne and Dany had set up a charity – the Dwayne Johnson ROCK Foundation – dedicated to improving the lives of children across the USA. In its first year it focused on working with at-risk and terminally ill children. Since then, it has expanded its mission to include education and childhood obesity programmes.

He supports other charities too, and he's also stepped in to help some more unusual causes:

⭐ In 2007, Dwayne and Dany gave $1 million to their old university's Football Facilities Renovation Fund (the largest ever donation from a former student to the university's athletic department). By way of thanks, the Hurricanes renamed their football locker room in his honour.

⭐ In November 2015, Dwayne heard about a shelter puppy that needed treatment to correct its heart murmur. It just so happened the puppy had been named after him. Dwayne donated $1,500.

Waking Up With The Rock

Dwayne's been involved in some unusual business projects too. For example, there was . . .

THE ROCK CLOCK

It was an iPhone app that woke up users with exclusive motivational and inspirational video messages from Dwayne himself.

The 25 ringtones were all created by Dwayne and included:

⭐ A simple beep, beep, beep.

⭐ Dwayne's dogs howling.

⭐ Dwayne singing:

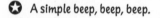

OooooWWW!

Good Morning, sunshine! ♪

Users got to sync their alarms with Dwayne's – to get up at 4 a.m.!

Then they got to set themselves a goal, with encouragement from Dwayne:

You can do this!

THE ROCK CLOCK
ROCK TIME
4:00AM
BEACH JAMS
SHREDDED
BAMF

The tough bit: There was no snooze button!
Users had to get out of bed when Dwayne told them to!

The clock hit the market in 2016, the same year Dwayne launched his own YouTube channel (he's currently got a whopping 5.74 million subscribers!). The channel features his very own cooking show called *What The Rock is Cooking* – remember his famous wrestling catchphrase? It features some of The Rock's favourite recipes.

Dwayne doesn't actually do any of the cooking on the show (could it be he's not a good cook?!), but in 2019, after Seven Bucks invested in his favourite ice-cream company, Dwayne used an alter ego 'Dwanta Claus' to invent two brand-new flavours: I Saw Mommy Kissing Dwanta Claus (rich whisky ice cream, peanut butter, chocolate-chip cookie dough and a milk-chocolate caramel-fudge swirl) and the Rock'n Around the Christmas Tree (Pacific Northwest spruce ice cream with raspberry jam, glacé cherries and gooey brownies).

Mmmmmmm . . .

FAMILY MATTERS

Dwayne and Lauren didn't get married until after their two daughters were born, tying the knot in 2019. They both dressed in white for the occasion and Dwayne was draped in traditional Hawaiian garlands, while his younger daughters, Jasmine and Tiana, joined in as flower girls. The ceremony took place on a cliff top in Hawaii and was so secret it happened **at 7.45 in the morning** (the equivalent of midday to Dwayne).

Dwayne and Lauren are good friends with Dany, who has also remarried. In fact, her husband, Dave Rienzi, works as Dwayne's personal trainer and her brother Hiram is one of Dwayne's very best friends and works for Seven Bucks Productions. He even took the photos at Dwayne's (second) wedding!

Sadly, in January 2020, Rocky Johnson died. For Dwayne it felt too soon; there were things he still wanted to say to his dad and now he'd never get the chance. But life has a funny way of lifting you up when you're down and in February 2020, Dwayne's 18-year-old daughter, Simone, took to Instagram to anounce some very exciting news: she had begun training sessions at the WWE Performance Centre in Orlando, Florida, and was well on the way to becoming one of the first fourth-generation superstars in its history.

Funnily enough, Simone claims it was not her dad who encouraged her to pursue wrestling, but Ata, her grandmother, who showed her wrestling videos when she was little.

Shortly after the announcement, Simone said: '*To know that my family has such a personal connection to wrestling is really special to me, and I feel grateful to have the opportunity, not only to wrestle, but to carry on that legacy.*'

Dwayne and Dany have both made it clear how excited they are for their daughter, while also stressing that the next part of her journey is entirely up to her. In the words of Dany: '*Your future will be uniquely yours to earn.*'

WHAT NEXT?

There are lots more film projects on the horizon, and Dwayne is about to fulfil a lifelong dream of playing a comic-book superhero in the film *Black Adam* ⑫Ⓐ.

However, Black Adam is no regular superhero. No, he's a DC comics supervillain and the arch-enemy of Captain Marvel. As the nemesis of the entire Marvel family, he's considered one of the **greatest comic-book villains** of all time. Dwayne's played lots of good guys, so he couldn't wait to turn 'heel' once again and get back in touch with his more wicked side.

Frustratingly, however, production on the film was forced to stop for a while when the Covid-19 pandemic hit the USA. Dwayne had only been back on set for a few weeks when he found he couldn't get out of his own home one morning – the security gate was jammed! He hated the thought of the rest of the cast and crew having to wait around for him, so he took matters into his own hands (literally!), by yanking the gate right off its hinges!

Dwayne topped the Forbes list of highest-paid actors in the world for the second time in 2020. Between 1st June 2019 and 1st June 2020, he earned an estimated 87.5 million dollars!

My dream of one day becoming rich has come true. And then some!

Dwayne is so successful, you might well be wondering what he'll turn his attention to next. He was one of the most successful wrestlers of all time, and now he's one of the most successful actors of all time. Is there anything else he could be massively brilliant at?

Well, Dwayne is also one of the few stars to have hosted *Saturday Night Live* an impressive five times. And that fifth show tackled something people have been saying he should apply his golden touch to for a while: the world of politics. It's been suggested that Dwayne should **run for US president**!

Dwayne's fifth *SNL* show took this idea to the next level, with Dwayne announcing he would run for president in 2020, with another five-time *SNL* host as his running mate: Tom Hanks!

It was a great joke, but Dwayne seriously **hasn't ruled the presidency out**. In an interview he said that it wouldn't happen for quite some time. *'I entertain the thought, and thank you, I'm so flattered by it, but . . . give me years. Let me go to work and learn.'*

In 2020, the Covid-19 pandemic started causing serious problems in everyone's lives. Shops, businesses, schools and colleges around the world were closed because of it, while the treatment of black people in America sparked angry protests by the Black Lives Matter movement. Dwayne felt moved to speak out, asking a simple question to his country's leaders: 'Where are you?' His despair turned to hope, in June 2020, when a high-school senior in Florida sent him a letter asking him to speak at her graduation – she even included a $7 down payment.

Dwayne was so moved by the letter that, by way of a reply, he posted a video online addressing high-school graduates across the USA, especially those who may not have the luxury of continuing their education at college. In it he answered his own question:

'Remember, to put your money where your heart is and always let your heart, mana and instinct be your guiding North Star. We must become the leaders we're looking for. And I can't wait to see the leaders that you and all your fellow high-school graduates become. Congrats, enjoy your summer, and keep being THE hardest workers in the room.'

And after that, betting companies gave **odds of 0.2 per cent** for Dwayne to win that year's November election – even though his name wouldn't even appear on the ballot paper!

DWAYNE'S TOP TIPS FOR SUCCESS

Whether or not he ever runs for president, it's clear that Dwayne will never forget his past: that eviction notice when he was 14, the shame of the failed football career that left him with just $7 in his pocket, the movies that haven't done so well . . . all of it has helped shape the person Dwayne is today. He really wants other people to learn from his failures and that's one reason he shares so much on the internet and in interviews. If you'd like to take advantage of some of his wisdom, here are a few of his top tips:

Don't let anyone hold you back

Always listen to the people

Stay focused and give everything to an opportunity

Work every day – harder than everyone else

WRESTLING TERMS

Babyface: A wrestler who is heroic and a good guy. They usually perform opposite heels.

Heel: A wrestler who portrays a villain or a 'bad guy' and acts as an antagonist to the babyfaces.

Feud: A staged rivalry between multiple wrestlers or groups of wrestlers. They are often worked into ongoing storylines and can go on for months or even years!

Gorilla position: The staging area just behind the curtain where wrestlers come out to the ring, named after legendary wrestler Gorilla Monsoon.

Locking up: A grapple at the beginning of a match.

Promo: An in-character interview or monologue, often designed to advance a storyline or feud at the same time as promoting (hence the name) an upcoming show or future segment on the current show.

Run-in: The unexpected entry of a new wrestler or returning wrestler in the middle of a match. Run-ins are usually made by heels, typically to further a feud with a babyface.

Sell: To react to something in a way that makes it appear believable and legitimate to the audience. For example, wrestlers may exaggerate the pain they are feeling for extra impact with the crowd.

Signature move: A move a wrestler regularly performs, for which they are well known.

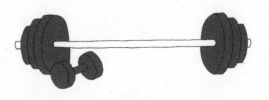

WrestleMania: A professional wrestling event held every year between March and April. It features WWE's superstars performing in a series of televised matches. At WrestleMania 35 in 2019, 85 wrestlers took part.

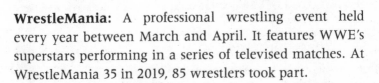

TIMELINE

The hard work never stops!

1972   2nd May – Dwayne Johnson is born in Hayward, California.

1986   Dwayne and his mum, Ata, are evicted from their apartment in Honolulu, Hawaii.

1990   Dwayne moves to Florida to attend the University of Miami and play for their football team: the Hurricanes.

1995   After graduating from university, Dwayne moves to Calgary, Canada, to join the Canadian Stampeders football team – two months later they let him go. He arrives back in Florida with only seven dollars to his name! That's when Dwayne decides to start training to be a wrestler.

1996   10th March – Dwayne competes in his first important wrestling match in Texas, in front of Vince McMahon (founder and owner of the WWE). The WWE offer Dwayne a contract, and he moves to Memphis, then Connecticut, to train with the United States Wrestling Association. He joins the WWE main roster and debuts on *Monday Night Raw*, the TV show hosted by World Championship Wrestling. Under the name Rocky Maivia, Dwayne takes part in the 1996 Survivor Series of wrestling matches and goes on an international tour.

1997   13th February – Dwayne becomes the youngest wrestler ever to win the Intercontinental Championship. 3rd May – Dwayne and Dany marry. Dwayne joins the Nation of Domination. He turns from 'babyface' to 'heel' – and changes his wrestling name to 'The Rock'.

1999   *The Rock Says . . .* – Dwayne's autobiography – becomes a *New York Times* bestseller. Dwayne has his first professional acting experience: playing his own dad on *That '70s Show*.

2000   Dwayne hosts US comedy sketch show, *Saturday Night Live*, and does a great job.

2001   Dwayne makes his Hollywood debut in *The Mummy Returns*. Simone, Dwayne and Dany's first daughter, is born.

2002   *The Scorpion King* is released: Dwayne's first leading role in a movie.

2004 As his contract with WWE expires, Dwayne says goodbye to wrestling (for now).

2006 Together with Dany, he sets up the Dwayne Johnson ROCK Foundation.

2007 Dwayne and Dany donate $1 million to their old university's Football Facilities Renovation Fund. The Miami Hurricanes rename their football locker room in Dwayne's honour.

2008 Dwayne and Dany get divorced . . .

2012 . . . then set up the Seven Bucks production company together.

2013 A bumper year for Dwayne – he appears in five films. This year, filmgoers spend more money watching Dwayne in action than any other actor in the world.

2015 Dwayne and his new partner, Lauren Hashian, have their first daughter, Jasmine.

2016 Dwayne has his first Disney role: voicing Maui in *Moana*.
He also co-produces and stars in *Jumanji: Welcome to the Jungle*, which would be released the following year.
Dwayne's YouTube channel, iPhone alarm clock app and 'Project Rock' partnership with athletic brand Under Armour are launched.

2017 Dwayne is awarded a star on the Hollywood Walk of Fame.

2018 Tiana, Dwayne and Lauren's second daughter, is born.

2019 In a secret ceremony in Hawaii, Dwayne and Lauren get married.

2020 Dwayne tops the Forbes list of highest-paid actors in the world for the second time. He shows no sign of slowing down . . . it's even been suggested he should run for president of the United States at some point in the future!

GLOSSARY

box office
The place where tickets are sold at a cinema. If a film is a 'box-office hit', it means lots of tickets were sold and the film was a huge success.

CGI
Computer-generated imagery is a type of computer software that creates special visual effects that can replace live action.

charisma
A personal quality similar to charm.

demigod
A character who is part god, part human.

dignitary
Someone who has an important, respected position in society.

eviction
When someone is forced to leave their home, usually because they can't pay the rent.

faction
A small group within a larger organization.

heritage
Values, traditions, languages and other elements of a culture belonging to a specific society, that are passed down through the generations.

high-grossing
Making a lot of financial profit.

intercontinental
Involving two or more continents.

opponent
Someone who competes against another person or team. (The Rock's 'opponents' were the people he wrestled against.)

peptalk
A short, uplifting talk intended to encourage people to work hard and try their best.

physiology
The study of how living things and bodies function.

physique
The structure or appearance of someone's body.

Polynesian
To do with Polynesia: a group of over 1,000 islands in the Pacific Ocean, including Hawaii.

producer
The person responsible for all aspects of making a movie, from sourcing a story, to appointing a director, to organizing the finances and distributing the finished film.

rookie
Somebody who is just starting a job or experiencing something for the first time.

roster
A list of people who belong to a group or team. In sport, it might be a list of people available to take part in a game.

scout
Someone who looks for, and tries to recruit, people with skills that are suited to a specific job, usually in sport or entertainment.

segment
A short part of a television or radio programme, which has a particular focus or theme.

skit
A short comedy sketch.

spontaneous
Something that is unplanned.

stagehand
Someone who moves props or scenery before, or during, a performance.

steroid
Medication that can increase muscle mass and improve athletic performance.

testosterone
A hormone thought to give men and male animals their masculine characteristics.

vandalism
The deliberate damage or destruction of somebody else's property or belongings.

versatility
The ability to adapt to different situations.

The show must go on!

INDEX

Use these pages for a quick reference!

A

Andre the Giant 100
animations 121–2
Atlas, Tony 13
Attitude Era 93–4
Austin, 'Stone Cold' Steve 80–1, 94–5
autobiography 96

B

babyface fire 78
Ballers 120–1
Bethlehem, Pennsylvania 22–7, 33
birth 12
Black Adam 142
Black Lives Matter 144
bodybuilding 9
boxing 10
Brooklyn Brawler (Steve Lombardi) 64, 65, 67–8, 69
bullying 21
Buono, Wally 51
business projects 137–9

C

Calgary Stampeders 51–3, 119
Canadian Football League (CFL) 51
Candido, Chris 69, 70
Chainz 86
charities 136–7
childhood 7, 17–18, 21, 133
college football 28, 29–32
costumes 63, 65, 76, 88
Covid-19 144
crime 7, 22, 131
Crush 78–9
Cwik, Jody 25–7

D

Diesel, Vin 112
diet 114, 117, 118
divorce 110, 125
dress style 134–5
drugs 24
Dwayne Johnson ROCK Foundation 136

E

education 7, 21, 22–7, 38–40, 45, 50
Emanuel, Ari 111
Erickson, Denis 34
eviction notice 8, 22, 145

F

Faarooq 85, 86
fame 96, 97, 99, 132, 133
Fast Five 112
Fast and Furious 6 115
Fighting with My Family 130–1
films 10, 99, 100, 103–8, 109–13, 121–2, 126–32, 136, 142, 145
fitness regime 10, 23–4, 58, 117–18
Flair, Ric 19, 20
football
   Dwayne's career 26–40, 44–5, 48–53, 120, 145
   positions 34–5
Frankensteiner 69–70

G

Garcia, Dany (1st wife) 42–4, 47, 51, 54, 60, 61–2, 70, 80, 82–4, 97, 110–111, 119, 136, 137, 140, 141
Garcia, Hiram 140
G.I. Joe: Retaliation 113
Goldust 78–9

H

hammerlocks 57, 58
Hart, Bret (The Hitman) 65, 66, 80
Hart, Owen 73, 80, 94
Hashian, Lauren (2nd wife) 125–6, 139–40
Hawaii 7, 21, 22, 127, 139
headlocks 57, 58
Hogan, Hulk 60, 100
Hollywood 10, 99, 103–8, 111, 132
honours and awards 27, 107, 133

I

ice-cream 139
injuries 37–8, 44, 48–9, 61
Intercontinental Championship 80–1, 94

J

Johnson, Ata (née Maivia) (mother) 7–8, 16–17, 21, 31, 40, 44, 47, 59, 79, 97, 141
Johnson, Jasmine (daughter) 126, 139
Johnson, Jimmy 30
Johnson, Rocky (father) 10, 12–18, 19, 21, 40–1, 44, 55–6, 57, 59, 60–1, 75, 79, 80, 96–7, 100
Johnson, Simone (daughter) 97, 140–1
Johnson, Tiana (daughter) 126, 139
Jumanji: Welcome to the Jungle 126–8

K

Karmelowicz, Bob 31–2, 38–9, 40
Kavana, Flex 71, 75

M

McMahon, Vince 19, 62, 67, 70, 132
Madison Square Gardens (New York) 74–9

Maivia, Lia (grandmother) 12, 16–17, 44
Maivia, Peter (grandfather) 12, 13–17, 44, 75, 122, 123
Maivia, Rocky 59, 75–82, 85–8
Maryland, Russell 36
Memphis 70, 71, 73, 96
Meng 63
merchandise 96, 135
Miami Hurricanes 30–40, 42, 45–9, 137
Moana 121–2, 125
Monday Night Raw 88, 92–3, 95
Monday Nitro 92
Moss, Larry 106
The Mummy Returns 10, 103–5
Muraco, Magnificent 19, 20

N

name 59, 62, 67, 70–1, 75–6
The Nation of Domination 85–7
National Football League (NFL) 28–9, 49, 54, 120–1

P

pager incident 95
Paige 130–1
Pain & Gain 113, 114
Patterson, Pat 59, 60, 62, 73
People's Elbow 90
People's Eyebrow 89, 122
personality, WWE 19, 60, 76, 82, 85–9
Piper, Roddy 19, 20
presidency 143–5
Project Rock 135
promos 87, 90

Q

quips 91

R

Rampage 128–9
Reed, Tanoai 116–17
Rienzi, Dave 140
Rock Clock 138
Rock concerts 91
A Rock and a Hard Place 131–2
Rolex watches 97
Ross, Jim 85

S

Samoan heritage 14–15, 26, 83, 84, 110, 116, 123
Saturday Night Live (SNL) 101–3, 143
The Scorpion King 105–7, 109, 116
Seven Bucks Productions 119–21, 126–32, 136, 139, 140
signature moves 90
singing 102, 125, 126
size 114
Skyscraper 128, 129–30
Slinker, Ron 57
small package 68
Snitch 113
social media 136
Soul Patrol 13
spots 57, 58
stunts 115, 116, 129
The Sultan 81
Super Bowl 29
Survivor Series 75, 76–9

T

tag-team wrestling 13
tattoos 122, 123–5
Team Rubicon 135
temper 25, 46, 47
That '70s Show 100, 101
tips, Dwayne's top 146–7
Tooth Fairy 110
tours, international 80

trash-talk 19, 31, 76, 90–1
Triple H 81, 93
TV and radio 98, 101–3, 119–21, 143

U

Undertaker 65, 66
United States Wrestling Association (USWA) 70, 71, 73
University of Miami 30–40, 45, 50, 137

W

Wake-up Call 119–20
wealth 96–7, 119, 143
weddings 82–4, 139, 140
weight lifting 10, 23, 118
World Championship Wrestling 92
wrestling
    family involvement in 10, 12, 140–1
    terms 148–9
WWE (World Wrestling Entertainment)
    Connecticut training facility 73–4
    Dwayne's contract with 70, 108, 136
    Dwayne's debut 10, 74–9
    Dwayne's trial fight 73
    Monday Night Wars 92–3
    personalities 19
    planned routines 64–5
    popularity of 12, 59–60
WWF 59

Y

Young Rock 133
YouTube channel 138–9

Here's a sneak preview of first names:

Beyoncé
KNOWLES-CARTER

first
names

Beyoncé
KNOWLES-CARTER

Nansubuga Nagadya Isdahl

Illustrations by Tammy Taylor

Introduction – Beyoncé Sings A Song

THE PLACE: St Mary's Talent Show, Houston, Texas.
THE TIME: 1988.

The school auditorium was so hot Beyoncé felt she could have burst into flames. From her backstage view (poking her head through the curtains), she saw a sea of people waving paper programmes around like fans. There wasn't a single thing in the world seven-year-old Beyoncé could think of right now that would help her cool down, though.

With her heart pounding as loud as a drum, her nerves were almost getting the better of her. She wished she could disappear. But it was too late now. **It was her turn to sing**!

'Take a deep breath,' her teacher, Miss Darlette, told her as she gave her pupil's hand a squeeze. Then she pushed Beyoncé forward.

The microphone and wooden stand were only a few feet away from her, but they might as well have been on the moon. Beyoncé's feet felt like they were dragging through sludge, but finally, she made it. Now all she had to do was summon up the courage to sing.

Beyoncé was used to family singalongs at home with her mum, dad and sister. Those were always a blast. But this was her very first talent show . . . her very first time onstage in front of a large audience for that matter. It was new, terribly scary territory.

As Beyoncé stood frozen in front of the wilting audience, the music started. **And then a miracle happened**. *Poof*, like magic, her pesky nerves were gone . . . and something else, something much bigger, replaced them. Little Beyoncé dug deep down inside herself and, spreading her arms as wide as an eagle's wings, she found the courage to sing. Her incredible voice carried John Lennon's 'Imagine' around the hall, and the audience were suddenly wide awake, sitting bolt upright in their seats. Beyoncé's nerves were completely forgotten.

As the song drew to a close, the audience erupted. Everyone was on their feet! Disaster was well and truly averted, and Beyoncé was in seventh heaven. She'd won a standing ovation and totally stolen the show.

Her parents, meanwhile, were in total shock. They hadn't even seen their little girl rehearse!

That can't be our Beyoncé.

To finish the story, see first names : **Beyoncé** Knowles-Carter ISBN: 978-1-78845-042-